THE
Opposite
of Spoiled

THE
Opposite
of Spoiled

Raising Kids Who Are Grounded,
Generous, and Smart About Money

RON LIEBER

HARPER

An Imprint of HarperCollins*Publishers*

HarperCollins books may be purchased for educational, business, or sales promotional use. For information, please e-mail the Special Markets Department at SPsales@harpercollins.com.

FIRST EDITION

Designed by Lucy Albanese
Title page photograph by Hurst Photo/Shutterstock, Inc.

Library of Congress Cataloging-in-Publication Data has been applied for.

ISBN: 978-0-06-224701-8

15 16 17 18 19   OV/RRD   10 9 8 7 6 5 4

For Jodi and Talia, who spoil me . . .

Contents

Author's Note

This book is intended to start conversations about money in our families, schools, and communities. But it's meant to be only the first word, not the last one.

While I've made the basic assumption that most readers have household incomes above $50,000 or so, just about all the tips and ideas can work just as well for families who make less and for those who have millions at their disposal. Take these blueprints, make them your own, try different tips on different kids at different ages, and please let me know how it worked out for you. You can contact me through my website, http://ronlieber .com.

I use the first person singular and plural—*I* and *we*—and the term *kids* often in this book, for two reasons. We parents are all in this together, and I think most of us want the same things for our kids when it comes to imprinting good values, virtues, and character traits. As for the plural *kids*, it's just for convenience; as the father of one child myself, I know that not every family has two or more. Using *kids* simply allows me to avoid gendered pronouns like *he* or *she*.

I tested many of these ideas and first encountered some of the people you'll meet in the book on my Facebook page, http:// facebook.com/ronlieberauthor. Please Like the page to follow along as the discussion evolves in the coming years. Other ideas came from talks I've given for schools and community groups around the country and from my writing for *The New York Times*.

Every quote in this book is real, as are all the people who appear here. The incidents I describe are true as well, and there are no composites. In a couple of places in the text, I changed names or towns (but nothing else) when my subjects did not want to draw too much attention to themselves or feared embarrassing family members or friends. The names Magnolia Davis, Bramson Dewey, Lucy Gilchrist, and Stephanie Joss are not the real ones.

THE
Opposite
of Spoiled

1

Why We Need to Talk About Money

The responsibilities we never faced at their age and the power of real conversations

In the middle of 2011, in the space of a single week, I heard from two different parents struggling with uncomfortable questions about money. A national conversation about inequality—about who had money, and how much and why—was beginning. A presidential campaign the following year was going to turn, in part, on who could best represent all of America.

Nobody knew how large and loud the conversation was going to be. But a bunch of curious middle and high school kids were making inquiries as they read the news and connected it to strains in their own communities. Are we rich? Who do we know who is rich? Why did you choose your job when you could have chosen something else that would have let us have a nicer home and go on better vacations?

Their parents didn't know how to respond, and I knew right

away why they had come to me for answers. Schools aren't good at dealing with questions like these. If teachers answer them by talking about government and taxes and policy, the responses can start to sound political (and boring). If they respond by addressing individual behavior and ambition, the answers start to seem like moral judgments. No matter how it comes up in the classroom, kids come home and start sensitive conversations and the administrators' phones start ringing the next morning with parental complaints. At private schools, where there is more freedom in the curriculum, talking about money and social class is particularly complex. There, most families feel lucky to have enough money to send their kids to the school or receive financial aid to attend, but parents and administrators get flustered if anyone brings up the topic of affluence and its effect on children.

Big Questions, Strong Feelings

Journalists, though? We love uncomfortable questions. And starting the year before I heard from the two parents, I'd been collecting the gnarliest ones that kids of all ages were asking about money. Each time I heard a good one, I'd put it up on *The New York Times* website. Why is that person asking us for money at the red light? Shouldn't we give our second home to someone who doesn't have one? Why don't *we* have a second home? Do you make less money than Daddy? Are we poor? Are people without nice clothes lazy? Will we run out of money now that you have no job? I suggested an answer for each one, readers pitched in with improvements, and everyone found it plenty useful. My own daughter, who is now 9 years old, was asking some of those questions herself, so I was testing the answers at home as I wrote.

The two parents who contacted me had been following these conversations online. And they had a challenge for me, disguised as an invitation. Would I speak to two groups of parents at their children's schools and give them ideas about how to talk to their kids about money? And could I please keep in mind that some of the families with more money than average were starting to feel demonized and those with less were feeling like their noses were being rubbed in everyone else's affluence? It would help, they added, if I could discuss the issues in a way that would not leave everyone in the room feeling resentful or inadequate.

Instantly, I said yes. There aren't that many fundamentally new challenges in the worlds of parenting or money, but this felt like one of them. And it was new for a couple of reasons.

In the past few decades, scholars have piled into a field that has come to be known as behavioral economics. If you've read any of the *Freakonomics* books, you know what this is about. Human quirks and emotions have a profound impact on economic decisions, from governments right on down to individuals. A ton of feelings are tied up in the decisions we make about our money and the amount we earn and have at any given moment. On one hand, there's often pride and joy and excitement about the things we're able to afford. But sometimes doubt and shame and embarrassment and envy creep in. Most people who read their credit or debit card statements carefully each month have felt many of these feelings at least once. And as I've discovered in my decade of writing about money for *The Wall Street Journal* and *The New York Times*, learning to recognize and control these emotions is the most important factor in picking the right mutual fund and shopping for a mortgage. It's feelings, after all, that drive bad behavior and lousy decision making.

I knew I could help parents with the basics of allowances and teenage spending guidelines. But any conversation about money also had to consider the emotional context—the wave of mixed feelings almost all of us experience about the money we have and what others around us spend. People are not dispassionate about money, and they're certainly not calm and rational about their kids. This potent mix, then, often makes it incredibly hard for parents to talk openly and honestly with their children about the topic.

The subject is complicated no matter what the socioeconomic level of a family. Affluent parents with more money than they need to live on will, by definition, be setting artificial limits with their children almost every day. As a result, their decisions about how much to spend on the younger ones and when to cut the teenagers off are more emotional than financial. Middle- and working-class parents often grapple with the practical challenge of living paycheck to paycheck while trying to provide their children with as much enrichment and fun as possible. But emotions come into play here, too, when children ask questions about why their family doesn't have more money, and the inquiries sound like accusations to their parents.

The New World of Money

When considering what to say to the parents who invited me, I wanted to start by reminding them of the fundamentally new challenges that are affecting our kids today and that will continue to affect them in the years ahead. It begins with social media, which is often an engine of envy for middle school and high school students. Children who are still fine-tuning their personalities put the best version of themselves out into the semipublic sphere, and all too often it's a chronicle of who has what and is doing what cool thing with whom in a locale that not everyone else can afford or may be invited to. Parents want to offer counterprogramming, but it's hard to fight the torrent of longing that frequent access to social media can inspire.

Our children will also be facing college costs that we could never have imagined when we were teenagers. A college education now starts at $100,000 for a flagship state university and rises from there to at least $250,000. This is an enormous sum even for families who can afford it; it's nearly unreachable for those who aren't able to save much money ahead of time. Sure, some kids will live at home or start in community college and end up paying less. Others will qualify for financial aid based on their family's need or their own merit. Better-off families may not qualify for much aid though. Meanwhile, parents who can't write $50,000 or $60,000 checks each year (or even $25,000 ones) often let their children decide whether to take on the student loan debt that will be necessary to pay the tuition bills.

It's easy to see why parents can't bring themselves to stop their children from borrowing money to go to college. No one wants to deny a child the opportunity to attend a dream university. Here's the problem though: The people making the final decision about whether to take on tens of thousands of dollars of student loan debt are mere teenagers. Figuring out how much to pay for a college education is one of the biggest financial decisions people make in their lifetime, and parents often leave the final call to a 17-year-old who has never purchased anything more expensive than a bicycle. There is really only one word for this state of affairs: lunacy.

After college, our children will enter a world very different from the one that new adults entered a generation or two ago. Health insurance and retirement savings are now largely the responsibility of workers and not employers. Instead of employers paying into a pension plan and providing coverage for illness and injury, individuals now save mostly via 401(k)s and other plans and pay for part or all of their health insurance premiums. This shift—moving the risk and the economic burden from employers to workers—has taken decades to unfold, but it's now nearly complete. What it means for our kids is hundreds of dollars out of their early paychecks to pay for things that the government now requires (health insurance) and that are all but essential (retirement savings), given how little income Social Security ultimately replaces.

For people who graduate from college with student loans, however, the debt payments may also eat up hundreds of dollars each month. While federal programs exist that reduce student loan payments and health insurance premiums for people with lower incomes, saving any money for retirement on entry-level salaries is extraordinarily difficult. And if they can't afford to save anything during their 20s, the effect of those lost savings can mean many more years on the job when they're in their 60s or 70s.

This shift in the burden has created an increased urgency around winning in your 20s financially, of not falling so far behind on retirement savings or a down payment fund that you'll end up having to work or rent forever. Young adults need to know how to save at 22 and have the habits to follow through with it. And picking the right college is only the first in a series of bewildering choices. They will need to pick the right retirement investments. They will need to select the proper insurance plans. And they will need to do so amid an explosion of products and people seeking to help them navigate this changed world. Many of these advisers do not have our children's best interests at heart, but by the time they're in their 20s, we may not be able to look over their shoulder and help them make the right choices.

So what we teach our children about money before then is crucial. It will quite literally *count* as they struggle to compare the right numbers and set themselves up for adulthood. It's unnerving imagining them trying to sort all this out on their own absent any help from us beforehand.

As for those parents who wanted me to come speak, those new developments were the things they worried about when they looked toward their children's future. They genuinely fear that their children may experience downward mobility. One comparison of the earnings of midcareer parents between 1978 and 1980 to what their kids were making between 1997 and 2009 is particularly enlightening: For parents in the top 10 percent of income—about $140,000 in today's dollars—just 20 percent of their children ended up in the bottom half of the income tables once they were midway through their own careers, earning about $52,000 or less.

Still, parents don't always have rational responses to those relatively low odds, seeing the one in five chance of slipping instead of the four in five chance of staying in the upper half of American earnings. We all want to protect our kids from every possible tumble down the socioeconomic class ladder. A 20 percent chance of ending up a bottom 50 percenter frightens us, even if they do choose the career that lands them there. Many of us are still shell-shocked from a financial crisis that made it clear how many grown-ups have it all wrong, from the millions of people who borrowed more money than they should have to the mortgage bankers who egged them on to the investment bankers who turned their loans into securities that they knew would blow up. Something had gone missing in the way many of these people were raised. But what was it?

Silence Around Money:
Blatant Institutional Adultism

Those parents who called me couldn't diagnose the problems, but they knew they were ready to discuss them. Talking about it sounds kind of basic, but it turns out to be crucial, given the epidemic of silence around money that persists within many families and otherwise close-knit communities. Many people who live paycheck to paycheck include their kids in daily money conversations out of necessity. But far too many parents avoid the topic altogether when there is enough money for every basic need plus most of the sneakers and costumes and lessons and electronic equipment that their children want.

This silence happens for a number of reasons, but there's one we should dispense with straightaway: The fear that talking about money too much will produce money-grubbing kids. Nan J. Morrison, who runs the Council for Economic Education, summed up the misconception best when she complained about the persistent parental belief that too much conversation about money actually *subverts* kids' values. It's as if it were somehow dirty and not an essential part of daily life.

Not only is this fear of money-grubbing kids wrongheaded, but older kids see right through the silence that results and find it completely demeaning. In 2013 I heard a young man named Jacob Swindell-Sakoor speak at a conference of educators and students outside Seattle. A mere high school sophomore, he delivered one of the keynote addresses in front of at least 2,000 people. In it, he called out all the grown-ups who brush kids off when they persist with their questions about money. "As our elders, it's completely irresponsible, and it's just blatant institutional adultism," he said, as the crowd exploded with whoops and whistles. "I say this because I hear it every day. 'You're the future of this and that, Jacob. You're the torchbearer.' But how can we be the future if you're not going to teach us about money, which *is* our future?"

Middle school and high school students like Jacob want to make money a focus, not a fetish. But one of the quickest ways to get them obsessing over it is to treat it like a family secret.

The parents who had invited me to speak at their schools did, in fact, want to talk out loud about things that matter, even if they were a bit uncomfortable doing so. Still, I knew their school communities encompassed a wide variety of incomes and an equally diverse set of feelings about money. What did they have in common? There was one thing I knew for sure: Every one of them feared that they would somehow raise a spoiled child.

Spoiled and Unspoiled

When you ask parents to name the worst single word that anyone could use to describe their child, a surprising number of
them answer right away with the word *spoiled*. I hear words like
mean and *cruel* and *racist* and *violent* pretty often too, but not
as often as I hear the word *spoiled*. Unlike *mean* or *stupid* or
average (my mother's response, God bless her), *spoiled* reflects
parental actions or behavior that affects the child's developing
personality. Spoiled by whom? Spoiled by you, Daddy-o! Sure,
kids will regularly scream and bite and swipe things and be
cruel in the early years no matter how good a parent you are. But
kids are not naturally spoiled; they're born lovely and innocent.
No, spoiling is something *you* do to them.

So if spoiled children is one of the main parenting outcomes
that we are trying to avoid or solve, then what is the opposite of
spoiled? Most of us know an unspoiled child when we encounter
one, and we can call up an example or two in our heads. But I
wanted a clinical definition, and I wrote one based on the assembled writings of James A. Fogarty. He spent years traveling
the country doing continuing education workshops about overindulged children for his fellow clinical psychologists and other
mental health professionals.

Spoiled children tend to have four primary things in common, though they don't all have to be present at once: They have
few chores or other responsibilities, there aren't many rules that
govern their behavior or schedules, parents and others lavish
them with time and assistance, and they have a lot of material

possessions. A 1998 academic journal article using survey data from adults who had been overindulged as children went so far as to refer to parental overindulgence of this sort as child neglect, given that it can hinder normal development.

It doesn't have to cost all that much to spoil a child, and three of the four factors in my definition of spoiled don't cost a thing. Even that last one—the lavishing of possessions—can still be in play for kids who are far from rich, depending on how many relatives dote on a child. Parents of middle- and working-class kids have many of the same worries about materialism and entitlement, given that all kids are exposed to the same acquisitive culture.

Creating an action plan and 15-year schedule of counterprogramming begins with a deeper understanding of what the opposite of spoiled actually is. The word *spoiled* has no useful antonym, as it was used to refer to meat long before it was used to tag children. Meat that is not spoiled is fresh, which is not the first word that comes to mind when describing an ideal young adult.

So in addition to the four criteria identified above, I assembled a list of values and virtues and character traits that come closest to defining the opposite of spoiled, ones that collectively add up to the kind of grounded, decent young adults that every parent hopes to send out into the world. And as I stared at the word cloud I'd created, I realized that every last one of those attributes—from generosity and curiosity to patience and perseverance—could be taught *using* money. Moreover, my ever-growing list of questions kids ask about money that render their parents speechless—Will we have to move if you don't get a job soon? Why do Uncle Joe and Aunt Linda have such a big house?—all had answers that ultimately lead back to those qualities.

Rather than assuming that money talk subverts values or is impolite or impolitic, we ought to do the reverse and embrace those conversations in service of raising virtuous kids. So that's what I went to talk to those two sets of parents about, and those conversations led to this book.

Talking About Money—and Values

The Opposite of Spoiled is a generational manifesto first and foremost—a promise to our kids that we will make them better at managing money than we are and give them the tools they need to avoid the financial traps that still ensnare so many adults. The book will serve as a framework for child-rearing that produces grounded young adults with financial habits that reflect maturity beyond their years. Money is central, but it is also a teaching tool that uses the value of a dollar to instill in our children the values we want them to embrace. These traits— curiosity, patience, thrift, modesty, generosity, perseverance, and perspective—don't belong to any one religion, region, or race. A few of our kids are already set for life financially, but most of them have no clue how much money they'll have when they grow up. Their financial status is fluid but their financial values should not be.

The list of values and virtues and character traits I compiled is a diverse one. Kids are ready to wrestle with them at different times, and children of different ages may begin to engage with them at entirely different ages. Plus, every child is different, so they'll respond to your tactics and strategies in a variety of unique ways. Still, we all need to know when and how to begin to introduce the topics, so I sought out a number of social scientists—people who have devoted their lives to studying kids' curiosity, patience, and character education and have run study after study about allowance and materialism and affluence. In each of the chapters, I'll introduce you to some of their best work and explain how money can play a role in instilling each trait.

All that aside, everyday families and their stories form the heart of this book. In the course of my research, I visited Mormon families on dairy farms in Utah, shadowed ace recyclers who are children in a California junkyard, drank iced tea with wealthy families poolside in the Hamptons, met with immigrants on their coffee breaks who talk about money with their children every day, and hung out in the kitchens of private school parents who have trouble talking about money at all. I've been on field trips to pawn shops and payday lenders with working-class students in Ohio and sat in on workshops with New England teachers whose annual salaries are less than what some parents in their schools earn in a month. In Michigan, I even tracked down the young woman known locally as the Bloomfield Hillbilly, a kid whose family has much less than her neighbors in their wealthy suburb and is working furiously to make enough money to buy her own horse.

The foundation of the book is a detailed blueprint for the most successful ways to handle the basics: the tooth fairy, allowance, chores, charity, saving, birthdays, holidays, cell phones, checking accounts, clothing, cars, part-time jobs, and college. Running throughout each of these discussions are frequent nods to the underlying questions that parents have about money, from the toddler years until their kids go away to college: When should I start what? Where's the line between a want and a need? How much is too much? And how much is enough?

At every turn, I'll be reminding you that it's children and their curiosity that often drive the process. Their questions are penetrating, and the most thorough possible answers may not always be age appropriate. So the book explains in detail how not to lie while also satisfying the insatiable desire for information that may be at the root of questions about what parents earn or why some kids have more than others.

Finally, I want to help all of you recognize that every conversation about money is also about values. Allowance is also about patience. Giving is about generosity. Work is about perseverance. Negotiating their wants and needs and the difference between the two has a lot to do with thrift and prudence. And running through all these conversations is a desire for kids to have perspective—to know why they may have more than most people in the world but will probably never have more than every one of their peers. And why there's no shame in having more or having less, as long as you're grateful for what you have, share it generously with others, and spend it wisely on the things that make you happiest. It's true for our kids, but it's true for us, too.

2

How to Start the Money Conversations

Curiosity, lies, and the single best reply
to every hard question about money
(and sex and drugs)

The kids in the Kessel house in Topanga, California, get only a couple of hours of screen time per day, only on weekends. Kaden, at 13 the older of two boys, could while away that time on any given Saturday with a music tutorial on YouTube or an online game. But one day he set himself down and paid a visit to salary.com. There, he typed in *financial planner*, his father's profession. A few clicks later, he had figured out what his father, Brent, earned each year: $700,000. Or so he thought. The number was not exactly accurate, and Kessel's earnings vary from year to year anyway. Nevertheless, Kaden presented this finding to his father as if it were fact. He had wanted the information so badly that he sacrificed precious Internet time to seek it out.

Brent makes his living asking relative strangers for their tax returns and retirement statements. Then he tries to coax them into disclosing their hopes and dreams and anxieties about money. Often, tears flow in the very first conversation. But when his son wanted to have an honest money conversation, Brent couldn't quite bring himself to present an accurate income figure. "I've been avoiding it," he said.

Here's what this tale tells us: First, kids are intensely curious. Lest we forget, it's their job to figure out how the world works. Money is a part of everyday life, and it's one of the things that many humans value most. So of course children are going to seek out information about it any way they can. They'll ask Google and present their findings to us. Or they'll make their approach with their heads full of overheard numbers that are correct but incomprehensible at younger ages, or speak with great teenage conviction about inaccurate figures they've picked up someplace else. And they'll inquire about any number of sensitive topics. What do you make? Are we rich? Can we buy that homeless man an apartment?

In this chapter, I'm going take a look at the things that may be holding us back from talking about money openly with our kids and offer some tips for rethinking them. I'll also share the single best tactic I know for answering virtually every money question that kids are likely to ask. Then we'll walk through some of the tougher ones and consider how best to answer them.

Why the Silence

Changing the subject to avoid answering any of the big money questions is totally understandable, and it happens for any number of reasons. We don't know where to start. We're intimidated by the enormity of the topic. We're sheepish about not earning as much as the parents of our children's friends, and we don't want our own kids calling us out on it. We're keenly aware of our own undersaving or overspending or other financial challenges, so talking about money at all, let alone to inquisitive children for whom we are supposed to be setting an example, is just too uncomfortable.

Many parents also believe that talking about money with children isn't age-appropriate. Their kids don't know enough math to add up bigger numbers, the argument goes, so it's best to just brush the questions off rather than trying to meet kids on their level. "None of your business" is a typical reply, which isn't particularly nice, nor is it particularly true. It is, after all, their business to be curious. And as members of the family, they certainly have an interest in its revenues and profits.

The appropriateness dodge may also mask a set of old-fashioned beliefs. Money is private, this line of thinking goes, and it's certainly unwise to trust children with any financial information. In Tad Friend's affluent family, which he describes in his memoir *Cheerful Money*, it was perfectly fine to engage in genial small talk about the cost of everyday items. But going any further simply was not done. "It is acceptable for WASPs to discuss necessary expenses ($18,000 for a new roof, the shocking price of heating oil) but not elective expenses, and never income," he wrote.

Silence also happens to be very convenient. It makes it easy for those of us who have a mortal fear of the money topic, or shame about our misuse of it, to justify not talking about it with our children, either. This reticence can be so strong that it sometimes manifests itself physically; I've had people break out in hives and burst into tears after just 60 seconds of listening to me make my case for talking about money more often.

Finally, there's the pleading defense of silence that so many parents have posed to me: Can't we protect them from all this money stuff just a little bit longer?

This instinct is loving, but it's also naive, and I'm not the only one who feels that way. Juliet B. Schor, the author of a book about children and consumerism called *Born to Buy*, described childhood innocence as "less a description of reality than a way for adults to project their own fantasies onto children." To Joline Godfrey, a consultant who works with many wealthy families, "protect" might as well be synonymous with "pretend" in this context. "Those children are out in the world, seeing things on television and on the iPad," she said. "So the fantasy that there is any way to protect children from anything . . . I mean, you have to arm them. This is human self-defense!"

Silence around money also happens to be a strategy that many of us learned from our elders. Old-fashioned parents who shut us up when we asked about money did this for any number of reasons. They may have been only one or two generations removed from an age when many American men didn't even tell their wives how much money they made or had. Or perhaps they'd grown up hearing stories about the Depression and didn't want their own kids even wondering about money, because wonder is just one or two short steps from worry. Their well-meaning clergy might also have convinced them that money was the root of all evil, and kids should come into contact with it only while putting money in the collection plate on Sundays.

So take yourself back to those moments when a parent could have enlightened you about money but didn't. Or when they were whispering so you couldn't hear. How did it make you feel? And do you want your kids feeling the same way, to know innately that money is important but also utterly off limits as a topic of conversation?

Instinctive silence around money may also be a response to its opposite—the loud fights our parents may have had over family finances. Those arguments can imprint specific lessons: Money is bad. Money is scary. There isn't enough money. Talking about money leads inevitably to strong feelings and conflict. These conclusions may be true in certain contexts but they don't have to be if we talk about the topic with care. So we should try not to pass these beliefs on to our children.

No Lying

Because money is so fraught, it may feel right to lie sometimes, particularly when children persist with unreasonable demands or ask the wrong questions at the wrong time. Perhaps the most common fib is "We can't afford it." Another untruth is "I don't have any money," though it's becoming slightly less common as kids get wise to the purchasing power of the debit and credit cards in our wallets. "Not now" is the most common brush-off from parents who don't want to bother explaining why they prioritize some types of spending over others, especially when children ask about it in front of other relatives or grown-up family friends. "There's no need to worry" often isn't true and merely amplifies the anxiety for a child who may have good reason to worry about the family finances in the first place.

At that point, many kids won't actually believe the lies, and the untruths can create new problems. James A. Fogarty, a clinical psychologist who has spent years traveling the country giving seminars to other mental health professionals who work with children, described the potential predicament this way: "The hidden message of offering the truth to children is that you and your children can work together to manage difficult issues. Children also learn that if they ever need a straight story, they can count on you."

Turn them away, however, and they're likely to go straight to their equally confused friends or engage in furtive Google searches. It becomes like a family secret, a vacuum that they will fill with whatever noise they hear out in the world. And they may stop coming to you with questions about many of the other important things they're curious about too.

When I speak to parents of teenagers and college students, they often grow a little weepy describing the moment that their children stopped coming to them daily or even weekly for advice or to ask big, cosmic questions. I get sad talking to them about it too. Like many of you, I imagine, I love nothing more than the look in my child's eyes when she's puzzling through an everyday mystery that's just out of her grasp and comes to me because she knows I'll stop everything to answer her question. Providing an explanation seems not just an act of teaching but one of protection. I don't ever want it to end.

Did You Ask a Good Question Today?

One way to make sure children know that questions are welcome is to praise their asking them so routinely that posing good ones becomes a habit. While celebrating the Jewish holiday of Passover a few years ago, we were reading from the Haggadah, a book of prayers and stories that Jews use to guide the Seder meals that take place on the first two nights of the eight-night holiday. The Haggadah was new; our daughter had put it together in Hebrew school. Inside, there was a short anecdote preceding the traditional moment in the Seder when the youngest child in attendance asks four famous questions of the adults in the room.

Here's the story that was in this particular Haggadah that struck me: "The Nobel Prize–winning physicist Isidor Rabi once explained, 'My mother made me a scientist without ever intending to. Every other Jewish mother in Brooklyn would ask her child after school: "So did you learn anything today?" But not my mother. "Izzy," she would say, "did you ask a good question today?" That difference—asking good questions—made me become a scientist.'"

All of this suggested an obvious new ritual: asking that very same question of our daughter at family dinners. Not only would it remind her to assert herself in the classroom, but it would reinforce the idea that questions were welcome—about money or anything else. Parents should try to bring the best question they asked that day to the dinner table too. When Katherine Simon, the author of *Moral Questions in the Classroom*, was evaluating a school for her own child, she tried to figure out if it would be a "place of intrigue." I love that word, because it suggests a sort of provocation. We should want our homes to be places of intrigue too.

Isidor Rabi died in 1988, but I figured his daughters might have some advice about how to promote curiosity in our own homes. It turns out, however, that Rabi never asked his daughters the very question that his mother deployed to inspire him. "He told the story about his mother all the time," said Margaret Rabi Beels, who was born in 1934. But because Rabi's scientific expertise was useful to the war effort, Beels and her sister learned early on not to ask too many questions about what he was doing all day. And while there were frequently guests at the dinner table, the girls weren't supposed to quiz them, either. "I remember Sir Robert Alexander Watson-Watt coming for dinner," Beels recalled. "He had helped develop radar, and they had smuggled him out of Britain or something. And we were told never to mention it to anyone."

Why Do You Ask?

Having sworn off silence and embraced tough questions, we can all but guarantee that our kids are going to ask a lot about money. We're going to try to answer honestly. But what's the best way to begin, once we get over the joy and delight in being asked?

In my years of research on the topic, I've determined that there is one answer that works best for any and every money question. The response is itself a question: Why do you ask?

This response is useful for many reasons. The first is a practical one. By training myself to respond this way, I've guaranteed one thing for certain: that I will have at least 10 seconds to think through potential responses, depending on the reason for the question. Yes, it's a stalling tactic. But be careful. There is a right way and a wrong way to question the question, given how vulnerable kids are to the belief that certain topics are off-limits. So I always try to say "why do you ask?" in the most encouraging tone possible. If your tone sounds suspicious, like an accusation or an expression of disapproval, it may shut down the whole conversation.

A child's response to "why do you ask?" often falls into one of two categories. The question may result from idle playground or lunch table talk. One kid says that his parents are rich or that the girl on the other side of the room has a parent who has a million dollars. So it's only natural that children will come home wanting to know how their parents stack up to some crazy number that originated with a fourth grader or a freshman trying desperately to get attention. But since the information that they're bringing home is usually wrong (or at least unprovable), it's often easy to redirect the conversation. We may know where people live and some of the things that they have, but we usually don't know how much money they make or what's in their bank account or what they had to borrow to buy their homes or their cars. That often ends the conversation there, since kids' curiosity may well be about exaggerated differences between their peers and themselves.

The second category of money questions springs from fear of some sort. Younger kids may overhear parents fighting about money or arguing about it with someone on the phone. Or they may take in fragments of an innocent conversation and blow it all out of proportion. Maybe something in a newspaper about layoffs or the economy catches an older child's eye. The "why do you ask?" strategy gives you a shot at finding the source of the anxiety. Once it's known, it often becomes clear that most kids, the younger ones especially, have no interest in the net

worth number they may have been inquiring about. They probably don't have much sense of what it means to be poor either,
even if they voiced concern that your family is about to be. They
just want reassurance that things are going to be OK—that they
won't have to move or leave their school or give up a pet.

Asking "why do you ask?" helps with nonmoney questions
too, by the way. I have a friend who was innocently sitting with
her father one day when her six-year-old son walked into the
room, fixed them with a gaze, and asked them this: "When are
we going to start having some sex around here?" At this, many
parents would stutter about, delivering a highly abbreviated version of the birds and the bees conversation. But the boy didn't
want sex, not with his mother or anyone else. He didn't even
know what it was. He eventually revealed that he had somehow
managed to steal a few minutes in front of a television while the
show *Family Guy* was on. It was there that he got the idea that
throwing the word *sex* around might get him some attention.

Girls, Too

As we move from why they're asking to how we're going to
answer, there's one other overarching issue to keep in mind:
gender. A number of polls and studies lay out disturbing parental tendencies. Parents are much more likely to talk to boys than
girls about investing, protecting their personal information online, how credit card interest and fees work, whether it's wise to
use check-cashing services and what a 401(k) is. Teen boys in
one Charles Schwab survey earned an average of $1,880 from
chores and jobs, while the girls earned $1,372. This seems to af-

fect expectations, too, since the boys believed that they would earn a starting salary of $79,700, versus $66,200 for the girls.

And what do girls get more of? Parents tend to talk to them more often about giving money away.

Grown women who recognize their own childhoods in this scenario tend to resent this treatment deeply. Women who learned as much as or more than their brothers did are grateful that their parents took this part of their upbringing seriously. So if your daughters don't ask the same impossible questions that your sons do, don't breathe a sigh of relief; all it means is that the girls are probably not learning as much as they need to know. These statistics are disgraceful, and our daughters shouldn't end up on the wrong side of them.

The Big Questions

So now we're ready. No silence. No lying. No gender preferences. A home as a place of intrigue. And asking why they're asking, every time.

Here's a list of the questions that many parents will hear at least once.

Are we poor?

There's a pretty good chance that this will be one of the first money questions your kids will ask. Parents who are in decent financial shape are often taken aback when it comes up. But starting in preschool, kids notice that other kids have things that they want to have too. This tends to weigh more heavily on their minds than the fact that they probably have some things that other friends don't. So the younger ones who don't know any better may wonder if being poor is the reason they don't have all the things they want. This is doubly true if their parents have recently turned down a request for a new toy or gadget, especially if that response included a fib about whether the family could afford it or not. If you ask why they're asking, that may be the reason. Still, this is a relatively easy question to answer for families who are not actually poor: People who are poor don't have everything they need, like food and clothing and medicine. We have those things, so we're not poor.

This gets trickier if you've just lost a job or have been without one for some time. Then, the inquiry may be more about what might happen next. Older kids may have figured out that sometimes families have to move to save money or because of foreclosure or so a parent can take a new job. Because the future is unknowable, it's probably best not to make any guarantees. But you can promise that no matter what happens, you have friends and family who are going to try to help and that you will do everything you can to avoid changing everyone's lives too much.

Are we going to have to move?

When an unexpected financial setback hits, kids tend to think about the most basic things first. So children who are old enough to understand that their parents pay a lot of money each month for the place that they live naturally wonder if a job loss will lead to having to leave it. It's best for parents to address this fear directly.

Anne Hickling and her husband both have degrees in developmental psychology, and they tend to tackle difficult topics head-on with their 13-year-old son and 9-year-old daughter. The death of her father led to many family conversations about the precise physiology of the end of human life, for instance. So when she lost her job of 11 years in May 2014, there was no false cheer and no lying when the kids asked whether they would have to move from their home in Phoenix. "We said we don't know," she said, "but that we were planning to stay here in the city and that they could keep going to the same school." The lingering question, which the family discusses, is whether they might have to sell their house and move to a smaller or less costly one, though it would probably be in a neighborhood closer to the public school they now attend. Staying where they are means much higher gas expenses, in addition to their current housing costs.

Right after Anne lost her job, the Hicklings also told the kids that they had some money saved up and that the company she used to work for was giving her some money to help. But they also warned the kids that the family would need to be much more careful about how they spent their money because they did not know how long it would take Anne to find a new job. In these sorts of circumstances, we forget how little children know about how the world actually works. "My daughter would ask me if I had gotten a job that day," Anne recalled. "She thought I would apply and just get one, not that it was competitive. The questions were ongoing at first, because she was thinking that there was this infinite pool of jobs, and it was just a question of my snagging one."

As Anne's unemployment extended into its fourth month, her children were growing accustomed to the fact that reducing expenses would make it easier for the family to avoid having to move. At times, they were disappointed, like when the family canceled a cruise with relatives. Sometimes, they pined for a first-run movie. But Anne's daughter also volunteered to sit out summer camp to save money. She and her father are big fans of Halloween, often dressing in coordinated outfits. They had grand plans for 2014 and had hoped to dress as Tinker Bell and Captain Hook, but she devised a backup plan to recycle her Little Red Riding Hood and her father's Big Bad Wolf costumes from an earlier holiday. Even as they willingly sacrifice on Halloween, however, it's clear that the kids are hoping things will change soon. "They recognize my job interview clothes now," Anne said. "And they get excited."

Any questions about living with less have the potential to sound more like accusations when parents have gotten divorced. After all, reasonable kids might observe that their parents have chosen to create the financial difficulty by living apart and creating another set of housing expenses. This can be hard for a parent to take but also hard to avoid, especially if both parents end up moving immediately to cheaper homes, forcing kids to shuttle between two new living spaces that both compare unfavorably to where they lived before.

Andrea Dutton, the mother of a 7-year-old daughter and 4-year-old son in Gainesville, Florida, addressed this issue simply and directly during her divorce. "I'm not apologizing to them about it," she said. "I want them to realize that the right decision is not always the easy one. I'd rather have them see that you can do the right thing and get out of a bad situation even if it means taking a hit financially. We're all so much happier now."

The three of them live in a rental home that is 1,000 square feet smaller than the home they once owned. Sometimes, Dutton's son will ask about the big house and say that he hasn't seen it in such a long time. "I want to go see it," he'll say. But Dutton doesn't have to explain why they can't go inside anymore. Now, her daughter takes on the role of the comforting grown-up and pipes up to respond. "She'll say to him 'I like this new house so much better, don't you?'" Dutton explained. "I'm trying to make sure that she doesn't feel like she has to take care of us too much at this age." (The week I finished the copyedits on this manuscript, the landlord agreed to sell them the house.)

Are we rich?

Why are they asking? With younger children, the question may not be about their own families at all. Instead, it's probably about their friend or classmate. While huddled over lunch, a gaggle of friends may have made a collective decision that a particular kid is rich, usually because of some article of clothing or the size of the child's bedroom or playroom or basement or toy collection. Having determined that someone they know is rich, they naturally want to know if they are too.

Once we know why they're asking, it's probably worth actually trying to define the term. This is challenging, since adults themselves don't agree about what it means to be rich. Ask some open-ended questions to steer the conversation. Does it just mean someone has a lot of stuff and a big house? (That's the usual definition for younger kids.) How much stuff? And what kind? Do we know how much the stuff costs? Try to make the end point of this line of questioning the fact that we can't really know very much about other people's money. We don't usually know how much they make at their job or whether a relative bought them the house and lots of the things in it. It's also worth questioning whether being rich matters much anyway. The most important attributes for friends and classmates are things like kindness, loyalty, creativity, and generosity anyhow. Kids who lack those qualities are no fun otherwise, no matter how much stuff they have.

Some children, older ones especially, will turn their sights on their own family. Maybe it's the new and bigger house that's gotten them thinking, or the last vacation. Or it's the comments their friends make when a parent drops them off at school in a new car.

One way to respond is by putting things in a larger context. They may already know from school or books that the vast majority of Americans earn more money and have more possessions than the majority of people on Earth. So we can start by noting that the United States probably qualifies as rich, and most of the children who live here without having to worry about food and shelter are well off. This may be too abstract for some children. In our immediate communities, after all, we often spend most of our time with people who are roughly like us. Some of our friends have a bit more and some have a bit less, but trying to place ourselves on a more-or-less-rich scale locally may be impossible or too subtle for younger children.

But money and stuff aren't the only ways to define rich. Ask kids if they have any other ideas for what the word means to them, or try some prompts if they're not sure. Perfect health? Living grandparents? Tons of cousins? Friends within walking distance? An amazing park nearby? Teachers and administrators who care deeply about helping the kids in their school? A god that they believe in? This is also your cue to tell them some stories about how far your family has come. A hardscrabble immigrant saga? A move from the farm to the city? Slavery to freedom? This is an especially enlightening conversation to have when grandparents are around to share some history.

This more personal context should help kids answer the question themselves. But that doesn't make it any easier for parents to spit out the answer that is probably true for many of us once we take all the data into account. While speaking to teachers and administrators at the Gordon School in Providence, Rhode Island, in the fall of 2013, Heather Johnson, a sociology professor at Lehigh University who is an expert on race and class issues among children, told her own tale of what happened when her third-grade son asked if the family was rich.

"My knee-jerk reaction was to be like 'No-o-o-o, we're not rich. Where did you hear that?!'" she said, describing how tempting it was to say those words out loud and how hard it is to acknowledge that she is wealthy by almost any conceivable definition. "I had to stop and remind myself that I'm out here giving lectures and that I can't do that. It was one of the hardest things I've had to do as a parent, but I looked him in the eye and said yes. And that was the end of it. You're supposed to wait for them to follow up and get into it, but that was it. He wanted to know, and I told him the truth."

Why can't I have it if I'm going to pay for it with my own money?

Insert the item that pushes you over the edge. Leather pants? Violent video games? Tattoos? Shiny automobile accessories that cost more than the vehicle? Even one more Lego? No judgments here. Your house, your rules.

Still, it's possible to wield authority in a way that doesn't make you an *authoritarian* parent. Such parents make demands but aren't particularly responsive, and kids may find their reign to be a bit arbitrary, given how hard it can be to get an explanation for various rulings. *Authoritative* parents are different. They, too, have high standards and plenty of rules, but they're also highly responsive. It's OK for kids to ask them for explanations and engage in debate. Decades of research have shown that children of authoritative parents tend to have better outcomes in all sorts of areas.

The tricky thing here is that even you may not be sure how to articulate why another American Girl doll is excessive or a belly button tattoo (and the clothing to show it off) doesn't feel right. Don't put pressure on yourself to explain it in the moment. But promise an answer eventually, sooner rather than later. Your child may not agree with whatever you have to say, but your well-chosen words may resonate much later, when your children are making much bigger financial decisions when they're no longer living under your roof.

Why couldn't you be an entrepreneur or doctor or lawyer or investment banker like my friend's parents instead of a teacher or social worker or psychologist, so I could have a horse or we could sit behind the dugout or we could have a weekend house near a mountain or ocean or lake?

Reading this question in a book may sound funny, but the only laughs are probably coming from those of us who have never had it asked of us. Hear this sort of question from your kid, and it sounds like an accusation. Our children have sat in judgment, and we've come up wanting in the provider department. If we have doubts about our career choice or trajectory, this will dig even deeper. Even if the idea of having failed them seems ridiculous, it's easy to blame ourselves for having inserted them into the types of environments where the luxuries they lack seem so important to them in the first place. And seriously, whose kids are these who care so much about things that cost so much? Ours? Really? How did that even happen?!

This type of curiosity is genuine, but it feels awfully aggressive. While we owe our kids answers to even the most obnoxious-sounding questions, it's perfectly fine to gather some thoughts first and wait until we feel calmer.

Joline Godfrey, who helps wealthy families talk more constructively about money, suggests one approach. It's born of her own nonlinear career path: She worked in a family dairy, married into a wealthy family in the timber business, got divorced, became a social worker, moved into human resources at Polaroid, taught at-risk girls, and then became a counselor to families at the opposite end of the income spectrum.

> The default is owning your own choices, as opposed to talking about somebody else's choices: "I could have made a different life choice, but I'd really be a grump as a parent because I wouldn't be doing something that is important to me. I'm a much more loving person because I have integrity and am true to myself, which doesn't mean that somebody else who makes different choices is not."

You're telling them that your values helped you decide some of these big questions, that this is a value you hold dear to your family. What's potent about that is that it's part of how a child acquires an identity, which helps dictate behavior. Values should drive behavior. And you've spent a lot of time thinking about what makes you whole as a human being. That's worth teaching.

Why don't you send me to private school?

This is another one from the question-that-feels-like-an-attack category. Parents often respond by saying that they can't afford it and that it costs too much money. But those are actually two very different responses. One of them is sometimes not true and the other represents a lost opportunity for parents to explain how they make choices.

Parents who don't think they can afford tuition at private schools can apply for financial aid, though they might not receive it, or enough of it. Those who don't apply can't be sure whether it's actually affordable, since they don't know what sort of aid they might receive. Some families who don't qualify for aid could probably cut spending elsewhere to afford tuition but choose not to.

Which brings us to the "it's too much money" explanation. This is a value judgment, and it may be the right one in any number of circumstances. Still, curious kids, particularly older ones, crave a better understanding of how their parents think about important decisions that affect their lives. They don't have much power, so knowledge is the next best thing. So we need to try, if at all possible, to give them a sense of how we make big decisions like this. Maybe the public schools are better or more diverse or both. Charitable families also worry about the impact of tuition on their capacity for giving. There is nothing wrong with any of these stances as long as kids get a chance to hear them out loud.

These conversations won't always be easy. Take one mother I

encountered in my reporting, who asked to remain anonymous because she didn't feel comfortable having her own choices laid bare and was taken aback at the specificity of her fifth-grade son's inquisition. She lives in an urban area filled with excellent public and private schools, and what follows is a condensed version of his interrogation.

Why were some of his friends able to go to private school, even if they didn't seem rich? The mother suspected that many of these kids had grandparents who were footing all or part of the private-school tuition bill, so she told him that.

Why can't Grandma and Grandpa help? They have two houses. That wasn't going to happen without their selling one house and then some, given that there were other grandchildren whom the grandparents would presumably want to help in equal measure. She explained this, too.

Isn't a kid's education the most important thing? This one was directed at the mother in particular, given that she'd recently scaled back to part-time work. She explained that she hoped that he would actually like the fact that she was home a bit more, helping out with homework and going on more school trips.

So why did we take that trip to Thailand? Indeed, an extended summer trip had cost about the same as a year of private-school tuition. But experiences are valuable, maybe even more valuable than an expensive education.

And travel is part of the family's shared experience. It's something they'll remember forever. So she tried to drive that point home.

This isn't even the whole transcript, and what lingered in the mother's mind for months afterward was her own question: *Are they really this on to us, at such a young age?* In fact, they are. By challenging our spending, they're challenging our priorities and values. But curiosity is just another word for trying really, really hard to figure out how the world works and how grown-ups make decisions. Getting angry or defensive about all of that won't make kids smarter. And while our answers may not always be satisfying, we ought to try supplying some anyway.

How much money do you make?

By now we know that "none of your business" is not the right answer here. But simply spitting out a number isn't usually the ideal response, either. Before there can be any financial transparency, there has to be readiness. Joline Godfrey, the former social worker and Polaroid staffer who now counsels wealthy families, said that she remembers at least one 13-year-old girl who was truly ready to have a mature discussion about her parents' income. Godfrey also shared the story of an attorney who called her, trying to figure out what to say to a 90-something-year-old client who didn't think his 70-year-old daughter knew enough about the real world to grasp the nuances of her inheritance.

Our own kids will probably ask this question before their teens, so we need to be ready with a response. And the best way to handle this is to explain that we may indeed want to share our salaries by the time they're in high school, but they first need to learn a lot more about what it actually costs to pay for the things that the family has and does. After all, it's not the income number that's important here as much as the context. What must we spend each month, and what do we choose to spend? How much is left over at the end, if any, and what are we saving that money for?

These are not rhetorical questions. Start with the smaller monthly bills. Cable. Mobile phones. Electricity. Teach them how to make a simple spreadsheet to keep track. If the family still pays bills by check, this is a good time to teach them how to write one, even if you think they'll never use the skill. At this point, they may bow out of the exercise, since it will start to feel like homework. That's fine; it's just a sign that their curiosity about your earnings is not that strong after all.

If momentum is building, however, start in with the insurance lesson. What sort of unlikely but expensive events is insurance for, anyway? Health insurance. Home insurance. Car insurance. Life insurance. Burial insurance. Maybe you have some disability coverage, too. If this line of conversation doesn't dissuade their curiosity, they're ready to know what your monthly rent, mortgage, or home equity loan payment is and how many more years you're going to be paying it. To engage them further, ask them to guess the amount of all these costs or do some research online rather than handing them the information. Explain your tax bills, too.

Now, for the rest of the spending: If you're a debit or credit card family, take out the bills and show them. Let them ask all the questions they want. Then, turn the tables. Can we remember a single thing we ate at that restaurant 7 weeks ago? If not, should we have saved the money and eaten at home that night, or were we traveling or busy and we truly needed to eat out? This sounds tedious, but there's no need to do it line by line all at once. Space out all the household bills over several months, or just go through a few. The goal is simply to help kids understand what things cost and what the family spends. This alone may give them enough information to feel satisfied about what the family has or makes.

Families with relatively pliant children will find that they happily play along, learning all the while and asking good questions about why things cost what they do (and perhaps making some uncomfortable inquiries about why we spend what we spend). Other kids, however, will be impatient, and they'll set out to acquire the household income information in some other way.

Which brings me to one of the best reasons to be honest with our kids about the family finances: They'll probably find out anyway. I know this because I was a snooper. I went looking for the tax returns, and I found them. I know other journalists who did the same thing when they were kids and thought that perhaps it was only those of us with the investigative gene who helped ourselves to our parents' financial information. But when I wrote about the "How much do you make?" question on *The New York Times*' parenting blog, *Motherlode*, in late 2013, a commenter told the tale of her snooping too. I tracked her down, and she told me her story.

At around the age of 10, Magnolia Davis's parents separated, and not long after, her father lost his job. His income declined by about 50 percent, and she had to change schools. All of a sudden, money—which had never been spoken of much—was a source of frequent conversation, conflict, and anxiety. So she began poking around the house. "When my mother took my brother for a lesson, I'd dig through papers," she said. "I looked through all the drawers. I did it regularly because there was so much secrecy." She did the same thing when she was at her father's house.

Magnolia's monitoring sometimes made her feel better. Her mother had been threatening to let the bank foreclose on their home in order to ruin her father's credit, but once she saw the mortgage statement she knew her mother wasn't following through on the idea. Other past-due bills would also be in the piles, however, which alarmed her. Neither the relief nor the fear changed her desire to know even more though. "I wish I could have seen it all," she said.

Some kids are just like that. Yours may be too, but perhaps not all of them. Magnolia's brother never expressed much interest in the topic of their parents' finances, though she would sometimes fill him in on what she had learned. Nevertheless, now that she's the mother of three small children herself, she plans to tell them everything they want to know about their family finances as soon as they're curious and ready to digest the information. "I'd rather just talk about all of it," she said.

Those of us who lead mostly paperless lives, in which most financial information resides behind passwords on the Internet, may not be completely shielded from the investigatory powers of curious children. The tricky questions about big numbers may start when they google their address for the first time. The first thing that usually comes up below or next to the neighborhood map is an estimate of the property's value from a site like Zillow. Try it yourself, so you can see what they will inevitably find. Once a child discovers this, they may show their friends, and soon all of them will have looked up every friend's home and those of their teachers and principals.

Also, if *you're* talking about local home prices, your kids will, too. Jim Dario, a TD Ameritrade executive, was driving around Mill Valley outside of San Francisco a few years ago with his wife and son, and his son's kindergarten classmate. When his wife pointed out a house that had just gone on the market, the classmate piped up from the backseat that the price was $1.8 million. Clearly, he'd already driven by with his own parents, who had looked up the price and discussed it out loud. This is yet another reminder that kids are always listening for a tantalizing piece of information that might be useful at some other moment.

Income itself is often publicly available too. Salaries of government employees, including state university professors and administrators, may be in a database that's reasonably easy to find. The same thing is true for people in the military or top executives at public companies. The five most highly compensated people at most nonprofit organizations also have their salaries listed in the federal 990 form, which older kids can probably find with the right bit of Google sleuthing. If any of this applies to your family, it doesn't seem wise to decline a question about a parent's income if an older child asks. After all, it would be difficult to justify a refusal to discuss a number that any random stranger can look up.

Income disclosure is also part of the process of applying for financial aid in college. Aid-seekers, including anyone who wants a federal student or PLUS parent loan, must fill out a form called the FAFSA. It asks for a bunch of information about your income and your assets. Parents sign it and swear that the information is correct, and the kids who are going to college put their signatures on the form as well. While some parents may simply hand the last page of the form to their child and ask them to sign it (without allowing the child to look at most of the income and asset information), doing so is in effect signaling that it's fine to sign important forms without knowing what is on them. Hiding most of the pages also implies a lack of trust, which is illogical. After all, the 17- or 18-year-old signing the form is getting ready to move away from home and spend piles of money on a college education.

Scott Parker didn't consider any of the above factors on their own when he made a decision to reveal his income to his six children. But he and his wife were intensely focused on character education in general. Like most Mormons, they devote one night in their calendar each week to "family home evening," when the eight of them would gather to engage in prayer, study, and other activities.

When Parker was growing up, his parents shared nothing about the family finances, even though they were open about everything else. "I had no idea what it would take to take care of a family," he said. "I felt it was a big disadvantage, and I wanted my kids to have a different sort of vision than what I had."

Then, one day he walked into a Wells Fargo branch near the family's San Diego home and asked to withdraw his monthly paycheck of around $12,000, all in $1 bills. The bank didn't have that many singles lying around, so it took a day or two for them to gather them and stack the money into $100 piles.

Parker, who worked in real estate, brought the stacks with him for the next family home evening and presented the money on the dining room table without much fanfare. "I definitely had their attention," he recalled. "And then I just started peeling it away."

He narrated as he went. First came the family's 10 percent tithe. Income taxes were next, followed by the mortgage and insurance payments. Then came the electric bill, car payments, gas, and groceries and other necessities. And that was just the needs—the baseline costs that were not optional. Next came the money for the weekly restaurant outing, followed by soccer and debate team trips and other activities. By the end of the presentation, there wasn't much money left at all.

"The first thing I thought they might think was that I made a lot of money, because they were sitting there with their mouths open the whole time," he explained. "But that was the last thing I was trying to teach. None of them, I was sure, had ever tried to add any of these things up. So I think it made a strong impression. I probably should have done it again later when the younger kids were older."

Their oldest son, Daniel, remembers many details from that night and also recalls the lengths his father went to to explain to the kids that it was a family discussion. Nobody needed to tell their friends about it. "I was taking a risk," Parker said. "But I can tell you that it never became an issue. I figured that whatever risk there was that they would talk about it was worth taking."

One of the things that gives parents so much reluctance to simply tell the truth about their income or net worth once kids are ready is this persistent concern that they will tell other people. But parents shouldn't underestimate how much kids just want to be like everyone else. Children of all ages generally don't want their peers singling them out as having more or less than others, so they may try harder than you do to keep the information private. Few of them want to be the richest kid or the object of anyone's pity.

When telling teenagers about household income, remind them that the information may not have much value to their friends in any event. Many of us live in communities or send our kids to schools where most other people are in a relatively narrow income band and not particularly interested in what other families are earning. Meanwhile, for those who are fascinated by this information, learning of it might be hurtful if they find out that they've fallen behind most other families in the neighborhood. This may be doubly true for friends of your teenagers, who probably don't need additional reminders that they're richer or poorer than everyone else and that people are taking notice of it. By explaining all of this, most teenagers will understand that there's no good reason to share the information with anyone.

Those teens curious enough to ask about the family income, ready to learn about the ways we spend it and wanting the information for the right reasons, deserve an honest response. What we make and how we make it is so essential to our lives that it seems wrong on the most basic of levels to shroud it in mystery and silence. And if we're talking about money all along—answering questions as they come and giving our children the proper context—knowing our incomes will just seem natural, and not a surprise or a privilege at all.

3

The Allowance Debates

Three jars, unpaid chores,
and a whole lot of patience

In the 18 or so years before your children leave for college, they are likely to want many of the following items: American Girl dolls. One-hundred-fifty-dollar sneakers. Then another pair six months later, when they grow out of the first pair. A second ear piercing. Beats by Dre headphones that will cover the piercings. Apps by the dozen. A microscope as powerful as the ones they use at school. Jeans with a price tag higher than in-state college tuition was 30 or 40 years ago. Concert tickets. Cars. An iPad. An iPhone. The new iPad. The new iPhone. Replacement chargers for the ones they lose, repeatedly. North Face jackets. A dog.

All the while, there will be many things you want them to do: Pick up a younger sibling from an after-school activity. Make the floor reappear in their room. Take out the garbage. Start dinner. Mow the lawn. Walk the dog. The dishes. Four loads of laundry. Grocery shopping.

Most parents consider these two lists and deliver a consistent message to their kids about the connection between them: Do the work, and we'll give you money to save up to buy the stuff. They call the work chores, and the money is the children's allowance. The lesson is that you can *buy* things, just so long as you *do* things.

It all seems reasonable. But there's something fundamental that we fail to stop and ask ourselves during the decade or so that we make our weekly distributions to our children: What are we really trying to accomplish with an allowance anyway?

When parents tie allowance to the completion of chores, they make work the primary focus, not money. But children have many places to pick up a good work ethic. Strict teachers, drill-sergeant coaches, and choral conductors will instill plenty of discipline. Homework is a slog that builds stamina over time. Most part-time jobs that teenagers take on involve a fair bit of drudgery, but they adjust and get dressed down by difficult bosses, and few of them ever get fired.

We should certainly do our part at home by making them do all kinds of chores. But they ought to do them for the same reason we do—because the chores need to be done, and not with the expectation of compensation. If they do them poorly, there are plenty of valuable privileges we can take away, aside from withholding money. So allowance ought to stand on its own, not as a wage but as a teaching tool that gets sharper and more potent over a decade or so of annual raises and increasing responsibility. This chapter is the user's manual for that tool.

Patience: Still a Virtue

An allowance helps kids learn to save and spend money, a skill they don't get to practice in very many other ways as they grow up. They are at a time in their lives when the stakes are pretty low, so the inevitable mistakes don't matter so much. Plus, the primary virtue of receiving an allowance is learning patience.

Figuring out how to delay gratification is a key part of handling money well, but the world now conspires against waiting in a way that it didn't when we were children. Movies are available on demand rather than on the waiting list from Blockbuster. Television shows need not have commercial breaks. Nobody has to sit by the radio until the song of the summer finally comes on. Information is at everyone's fingertips, so there's no more need to go to the library to figure out why the sky is blue or what sea otters look like when they swim. Homes have more bathrooms and telephones, which means less sharing and no waiting. Most of our kids have no recollection of having to wait to see what the photographs they just took are going to look like.

But collecting a big enough pile of money to do or buy fun things still requires some waiting when you're a child who is too young to have a credit card. And the patience this requires is associated with many good financial outcomes for adults. It's the rare study that tracks the same group of children well into adulthood, but a 2011 one out of New Zealand followed 1,000 people from birth to the age of 32. By that age, it was clear that those who had poor self-control as children were less likely to save money, have a retirement account, or own homes or stocks as adults than those who had more self-control. The low-self-control group also had more credit problems. Lack of self-control was even more predictive of money problems than their social class as kids or their IQ.

Teaching our children the ability to wait is a big part of our overall goal, and what's most important about an allowance is what will happen when they're too old to get it. We parents are in the adult-making business after all, and we should do everything possible not to squander the opportunity to build grown-up humans with 15 or 20 years of experience handling money. With enough practice, our kids can develop the kind of restraint that will keep them out of trouble while still allowing them to spend plenty on the things that give them the most joy.

Allowance: When, How Much, Where, How

So when do we start? By first grade at the latest, though there is no harm in starting sooner. If a child can count and is asking questions about where money comes from and what things cost, then it's time to begin. Kids who have gotten wise to the power of pestering parents to buy things are ready as well. Even if children seem oblivious to money, there is subtle power in having them watch their small piles of allowance money grow bigger over time.

The next task is to figure out how much money a child should receive each week. With children under 10, 50 cents to $1 a week per year of age is a good place to start, with a raise each year on their birthdays. We want them to watch the money grow and strive for a goal, so they should have just enough to buy some of what they want but not so much that they don't have to make plenty of tough choices. Starting low allows for more frequent or bigger raises if the initial amount doesn't seem right (and avoids a reduction, which can feel like punishment). Older kids will probably need more money, depending on whether they're paying for meals or gas or clothing, all of which I'll talk about in more detail later.

Once you have an amount, you'll need a system for tracking and storing the money. In my family, we divide the allowance into three clear plastic containers: one each for spending, giving, and saving. This is, in effect, a first budget. Splitting the money introduces them to the idea that some money is for spending soon, some we give to people who may need it more than we do, and some is to keep for when we need or want something later.

The Spend container holds money for occasional impulse purchases. If our daughter gets the urge for something small when we're out and about, we front her the money until we can get home and take it out of the Spend container. We don't have many rules for this money and consider it a kind of mad science experiment. It's fascinating to see what moves kids to want to buy something once the money is actually their own. They often want random junk, but this is part of the process of letting them practice. After all, how can we teach them to control their impulses until we observe them under real-world conditions with actual green cash?

Kids who are new at handling money will frequently engage in all sorts of ingenious antics with whatever money you give them access to. Take a boy I know whose mother asked me to keep his name private lest he be embarrassed when he's older.

He had received two $20 bills for his birthday and he insisted on carrying them around in a crumpled lump in his pocket every day despite his parents' protestations. They decided it would be a teaching moment if he lost the money, but he didn't (though it did go through the wash a few times). He was waiting for the right moment to use the cash, and it arrived one day at lunch when he decided to buy his way to the front of a long cafeteria line with one of his bills. Rather than wait, he handed a $20 bill over to a child at the front and cut in. Once he'd eaten, he used the other bill on the playground to buy a ball from a friend who had been reluctant to share it.

A teacher eventually got wise to the $20 bills floating around and made the two kids give back the boy's money. Which is really too bad, as it would have been interesting to know whether he felt days later that this was money well spent and how the parents of the newly flush children felt about the emerging underground economy at their school.

The second is the Give container. One way to introduce the idea with younger children is to talk about sharing. In the same way we share our toys with our friends, we also share some of our money with people who need it, except with money we don't expect to get it back. Talk about times they may have seen you give, to a person on the street or a collection plate at church. Ask them about the things they love to do, whether it's going to the park or the zoo or the local children's museum. Chances are, there's a way to give money to help those institutions, and most of them will have fund-raising staff who will be particularly excited to accept money directly from a child. This, too, is an avenue for teaching patience. Even the youngest children understand that the more money you put in the Give container, the more you can help. Waiting until the container is full before giving the money away will give them a real sense of accomplishment. Families who do a lot of volunteer work should talk about that, too, since money is not the only way to give.

The last container is the Save jar, and we consider it an imperative, a commandment of sorts. Save! But it's also a joyful exclamation, the sort of thing you'd shout before beginning a journey to a fun destination. One note: Younger kids can have a fuzzy sense of time, so any savings goal should be relatively short-term at first. By keeping the goals modest, there's a better chance of meeting them. Make them concrete, too; it can help for children to cut out a photograph or draw a picture of whatever it is they're saving for and tape the visual onto the container itself.

Keep things easy at first by putting an equal number of dollar bills in each container. Alternatively, divide things up so that you need only singles and no change, say, by distributing $2 each week for both spending and giving and $4 for saving. After a few years, consider allowing the children to decide how to divide the money. At that point, there can be an extra incentive for saving. Financial planner Brent Kessel and his wife pay interest on the money their kids save and that which they set aside for charity. Their interest schedule starts off quite generous—anything under $50 earns 50 percent each month. (Yes, not each year but each month; if only banks worked like that.) All money under $100, however, earns just 25 percent in interest, and the rate continues to fall as the balances rise. Eventually the interest falls to a 1 percent monthly rate on anything above a $2,000 balance. I thought this was a bit odd; why not pay even more as they save more to reward their patience? "I found they over-saved even with this schedule," Brent explained. "Which is why I dropped the interest amount at higher levels. They would have bankrupted me otherwise!"

Gifford Lehman, a financial planner who lives in Monterey, California, gave his kids a choice. They could pay a 15 percent tax on their allowance, which he would make them physically hand back to him to make it tangible. Or, they could set aside twice as much as the tax (30 percent of the allowance, in that case) and then collect a 100 percent match (turning a 30 percent savings rate into 60 percent). This might seem like a no-brainer, but it isn't always easy for kids (or adults) to be patient enough to wait around to collect on that 60 percent. The unspoken understanding in the Lehman household was that the matched savings was for goals that were years away. If the matching numbers are big enough, many kids will get in the habit, as Lehman's kids (now grown) did. And it's a useful habit, since employers often reward retirement savings in the same way in 401(k) and similar plans by matching some of the workers' contributions.

Whatever rules you set for spending, giving, and saving, starting a weekly allowance is a commitment, so it will help to get a few things squared away ahead of time. First, there are the containers themselves. I hate piggy banks, and the problem begins with the metaphor itself. Pigs are dirty, and they eat a lot, so piggish behavior isn't something to aspire to. And the idea that you're somehow a hog if you save money isn't accurate. Meanwhile, ceramic or metal containers are problematic, since we want kids to be able to see what's inside and watch it grow. Also, it should be easy to put bills in and take them out. Tiny slots or complicated openings that require folding bills into little squares don't work well. After trying a couple of different solutions in our family, we finally defaulted to the clear plastic bins that Rubbermaid and others sell as containers for cereal or rice, and our daughter decorated them.

Next, the money to put in the containers needs to be available on the chosen day each week. We did two things to make sure we had enough of the right bills on the right days. First, I started hoarding $1 bills, depositing them in a bowl in our apartment every few days. Then we joined the credit union at our office specifically so we can drop in any time and exchange a few $20 bills for a stack of singles. We also set a calendar alert for each Saturday morning so we would remember to distribute the money, though our daughter now remembers herself most of the time.

In some families, children may have savings accounts that family members have seeded, but they come with strict instructions that the kids aren't to touch the money for a good long while. Kyle Jones and his sister, Stephanie, grew up in Baton Rouge, Louisiana. His maternal grandmother worked as a housekeeper and earned $1 a day when she first started out. "If you think about that movie *The Help*, well, she was the help," Kyle said. Her husband died young, but she still managed to help Kyle's mother through college and graduate school.

Though her wages remained low throughout her life, she was careful with her Social Security check, and she had a bit of savings when she died. Kyle was 11 years old, and once the family paid the bills for the burial, there was about $10,000 left. Kyle's mother, Mary Louise, already had strict instructions about what was supposed to happen to it. "My mother had told me to take whatever was left and save it for Kyle and Stephanie," she said. "She didn't care about me."

So Mary Louise put the money away, and Kyle and Stephanie were only vaguely aware of it. They knew better than to ask for any of it either, even for college, for which they both took out loans. In this family, the money has a specific purpose. "The idea of creating generational wealth is something new in the black community, because there isn't a lot of old money per se," said Kyle, now a grown man living in Harrisburg, Pennsylvania, and working in finance. "I don't even think of that money as real. I get the tax form each year, but it's not for my everyday life. I need it for my next life. It's almost as if my mother has shamed me for it. It doesn't exist!"

Using the Bank (or Not)

After a few years of distributing allowance money and granting occasional raises, the sums in the Save container will start to get larger. Parents who remember their first real savings account at a bank may want to open one for their kids. But for children between 8 and 13, it may be best to wait. If we make them put their allowance money in a bank, where the balance is abstract and not visceral like a container full of cash, that account may begin to seem like a black hole for birthday checks, as David Owen put it in his book *First National Bank of Dad*. Savings shouldn't feel like punishment, especially when the interest rarely amounts to what it did back in the 1970s and 1980s. One alternative is to cash those birthday checks ourselves and drop them in the Save container, which ought to be kept someplace safe though easily accessible. Teenagers can make their own decisions about when to open a real savings account, say, when they want to start putting money out of easy reach to save for a car or college tuition.

Still, once kids have moved on to higher math, keeping their Spend money in a container no longer teaches them much about counting. At that point, going virtual may make sense. Sites and apps like Allowance Manager and FamZoo help parents assign and track both chores and allowance, whether kids have to do one to get the other or not. When kids want to use the money that the app is tracking, they can spend it online with parental supervision or receive the money on a debit card that parents load via their checking accounts.

Another option is to push money from our own checking accounts to a child's checking account at the same bank each week. Just make sure there aren't any fees for the small balances the kids will likely have, and turn off any overdraft coverage that would allow them to spend more than there actually is in the account. Credit unions and community banks often have lower fees than the branches of big national banks, and online banks like Capital One 360 and Ally offer free accounts with no minimum balance requirements. Some banks will let you electronically transfer money to accounts at other institutions on a regular basis without charge. Ask about this before opening a checking account for your child at a bank that is not your own.

As for credit cards, there's little need for a teenager to carry one unless it's strictly for emergencies. Why introduce them to the idea of spending money on a card that allows them not to pay the full bill each month and pay interest instead? Debit cards exist for a reason—to help people stick to a budget. New handlers of money need that help more than anyone, so kids shouldn't get in the habit of buying on credit too early, even if it is our cards that they're using. If parental convenience is the goal, we can give them cash to buy things they need or transfer money to their checking accounts so they can use their own debit cards. Then there won't be any way of spending more money than they have.

Wants and Needs (and Carnivorous Plants)

Wherever a child's money may reside, the urge to spend it will eventually arise. Which begs a basic question: What do we want our kids paying for exactly, and what sort of spending should we ban altogether? The answers to these questions will evolve over time, since we can't anticipate everything. Still, by as early as age 5, kids are ready to reckon with the framework that ought to govern a lot of their spending for the rest of their lives: wants and needs (and knowing the difference).

With younger children, the definitions can be relatively simple: We *need* food to eat, clothes to wear, a home to sleep in, doctors and medicine to keep us healthy, and a babysitter or after-school classes if there isn't a parent at home. Most families consider saving a need too, for the kids' college tuition and for retirement. A car may also be a need, and many parents treat books and charity or tithing as a necessity too. Then there are things we *want*, like treats, sports equipment, toys, local excursions, and vacations. These are nice things to have, the explanation can go, but we won't always get all the things on this list that we want, nor will we get them all at once.

It's also useful to have kids generate their own list of needs and wants at the outset of the allowance process, just to see what they come up with. Once they understand the concept, be prepared for it to come up at unexpected moments. By the time she was 6, our daughter had already figured out that our car was not truly a need, given that all three of us can use the subway to get to work, school, and most weeknight and weekend events. She explained this while we were giving a ride to a friend of hers whose family did not have a car and wondered why we did. By age 8, she was evaluating charities on the basis of whether they were delivering services that people truly needed, like life-saving medicine, or just things that were nice but not necessary, like public displays of art.

The want versus need test will inevitably come up as our kids get older and start to question the fairness of parental spending decisions. The very best question I've ever heard after one of my talks on money and values came from a stumped mother who stood up in front of her peers and reported the following: Her middle school son had asked her why he couldn't have a high-priced carnivorous plant terrarium, since his parents had bought Hunter boots for his sister. The juxtaposition was a great one, given that many parents are willing to spend as freely as they can afford to on tools for learning, and an interest in plants seems well worth cultivating. After all, kids *need* to learn; they merely *want* fashionable, expensive rain boots. I told the inquiring mom to let the kid have some Venus flytraps already.

The Lands' End Line

Clothing is, indeed, a challenging arena when it comes to defining the line between a want and a need. Peer influence and brand names begin to affect kids' thinking early on and often become more important to them as they become teenagers. Adults, meanwhile, may have their own flexible definitions of need, justifying more expensive clothing with the presumption that it will last longer or wear better.

As children get older, the easiest way to avoid whining and arguing while also giving them some say in the matter is to do two things: First, create a Want/Need continuum—literally, a horizontal line drawn on a piece of paper for the kids to see— with Needs at one end and Wants at the other. Let's say the request is for rain boots. Most kids need them, but the rubber doesn't get better when the price quadruples. At the left end of the continuum are the discount or used boots that may cost up to $25 or so. Label that end Need. On the right end are the Hunter or other brand-name boots that can cost well over $100. Label that end of the continuum Want.

Now, the big decision: We have to draw a vertical line that crosses that horizontal continuum somewhere between the low extreme and the $100-plus one. It's a sort of proverbial line in the sand that represents what we're willing to pay for a child's need (anything to the left of the line) and what we won't (anything to the right, up to and including Hunter boots). My wife and I are still debating exactly where we'll put this line and whether it will move to the left or the right, depending on the item. I'm making the case for a broad-based "Lands' End Line." If we adopt it, that means we'd pay whatever Lands' End (my definition of a suitably mid-priced merchant that sells quality clothing) would charge for any clothing needs, even if an item comes from some other designer or shop. Anything with a price to the right of the Lands' End Line would be a want. And if our daughter craved that item, she could pay, out of her Spend or Save containers, the difference between its price and the price of a similar item at Lands' End. We've found that grandparents will gleefully disrupt this attempt at standard-setting with spontaneous bursts of generosity. Still, as long as that doesn't happen too often the continuum will hold if we parents apply it consistently.

After a few years' experience with this continuum, middle school children can take over their entire clothing budget themselves. First, try figuring out everything they might need in the coming year and what the total budget will be, given where you draw your own Want/Need line. Then, hand that money over in a lump sum, perhaps as a separate prepaid debit card for them to use just on clothes. This may seem risky, given how many opportunities there are to make bad choices, but it's a powerful experience.

Cheryl Holland, a financial planner in Columbia, South Carolina, did this with her daughter once she was in high school. While she had fears of her daughter wearing flip-flops all winter after spending the warm-shoe money for a party dress, she let her make her own decisions. They made a list of the items she needed to buy but laid down no rules about what came from where. Sure enough, a lot of the money landed in the cash registers at PINK Victoria's Secret. She also outgrew the pricey jeans she had bought early in the year, and her parents declined to bail her out when her budget didn't allow for any new ones. Most kids will mess this sort of thing up, sometimes spectacularly, but they learn very quickly. That's doubly true if you let them keep any money they have left in the clothing budget at the end of the year, or roll it over into the following year's budget.

The real surprise for the Hollands was how quickly their

daughter became savvy. "She has become an excellent shopper, thinking through what she needs, watching for sales, and earning extra money for what she wants that her budget doesn't cover," Holland said. In fact, she's probably saving her parents money, because Cheryl has a tendency to spend a bit more in the interest of expediency when they're in the store together. "My recommendation would be that if a child is asking for responsibility around money, give it to them."

New Rules: Essay Tests, Push-Up Bras, and Inconvenience Taxes

So how far can we push these allowance principles? Some parents decide early on that anything and everything their child wants—as opposed to needs—is going to come out of their allowance. Parents who do this generally make exceptions for birthday and holiday presents and occasional vacation souvenirs but are strict with most other purchases. For instance, if the parents choose to take the family out for dinner, it might be up the kids to pay for beverages they want other than water. With this system, kids often get more dollars each week so that they can afford at least some of the things they want. This may sound harsh or cheap, but it all depends on the size of the allowance. What it actually does is give kids a lot more power and control and presents many more opportunities to learn.

Inevitably, disputes will arise about the precise definition of need, especially when entirely new requests come about. Bill Dwight, founder of the virtual family bank, FamZoo, has an elaborate exercise he's used with his kids over the years to settle these questions. Say they're interested in some new video games. They have to write a short essay explaining why. Meanwhile, with items like laptops, he sits down with them and figures out what a basic model would cost that fulfills their needs. When they almost inevitably want something more expensive, he'll agree to advance them the money for the difference and then dock their allowance for the next several months until they've paid back the advance. He charges no interest, as he believes that the pain of having bits of money drained from their allowance each week for a while is lesson enough.

Older children will eventually end up with money that does not come from their allowance, say from a job or a birthday or holiday gift. Once that happens, set some sort of policy on how much of it they can spend. Perhaps the rules are loose for gifts, and kids can spend most or all of that money on whatever they want. Some parents may want earnings from part-time jobs to replace allowance in the teen years or cover new expenses, for a car perhaps. Others may want their kids to set all that money aside for college. There are no right answers here, as long as there's a clear policy that you apply consistently and revise if the family's needs change.

We'll also need a list of banned items, which will change over time as kids develop new interests and companies invent ever more inappropriate ways to satisfy them. These are things that we won't let our children buy, even if they're using Spend money from their allowance or funds they earn from a job. Parents who follow my Facebook conversations shared their own lists of banned items with me, in case you're looking for ideas. They include, in alphabetical order: Airsoft guns, Barbie dolls, candy, the Claw machine at the arcade that fishes out stuffed toys (or tries to), dogs, hamsters, Heelys shoes, in-app purchases, iPhones, Legos (additional), motorcycles, Nike Elite socks, Oakley sunglasses, pocket knives, push-up bras, anything with a skull and crossbones, skydiving, tattoos, trampolines, and violent video games. If your child has you looking for evidence that at least one other mean parent won't let their kids spend their own money on one of these things, now you have it.

As for things you bought that they genuinely needed but subsequently were lost or broken, some ground rules are in order too. One way to reinforce responsibility is to ask children to contribute to the cost of repairing or replacing these items. With younger kids who don't have much money and are still learning to keep track of their belongings, a nominal contribution of a month's worth of Spend money toward replacements makes sense. Older kids can make a case for how much fault they bear in each situation and pay for all or part of replacements or repairs based on whatever judgment we render.

Aimee Sims, of Alexandria, Virginia, takes an additional measure with her 10-year-old son, which became necessary when he stopped worrying about losing things that he could replace out of his allowance. He didn't seem to miss the funds, so a more painful penalty seemed to be in order.

When he repeatedly misplaced lunchboxes, thermoses, and drink bottles, he simply borrowed his sister's. "Which was all well and good, until he started forgetting her thermos at school too," Sims recalled. "Now there's a tax. If you inconvenience someone else by being irresponsible, you pay $5 if you forget it, and $20 plus the cost of a new item if you lose it." The beneficiary of the tax is the person who was inconvenienced. And for whatever reason, it drives the boy bananas to hand money over to his sister, even though he doesn't mind paying to replace lost items. After he had to pay for about five thermoses, this seems to have done the trick.

Smartphones:
Usually Not a Need

With these rules in place and some experience setting and adjusting them along the way, it will get easier to make tougher calls around more expensive items like phones and cars. Let's take them in order.

We'll begin with a few phone stipulations. Kids need a basic cell phone, but smartphones are a want. And because smartphones are a want, they should pay for such phones and whatever extra data they use each month. Why do they need basic phones? Less for calling than for texting, which seems to be the default form of communication for everyone from kids to sports coaches. But nobody needs a phone that can handle apps, though there are a few exceptions. A school may insist that app access is necessary to complete class assignments, or a parent may have anxiety about not being able to follow the dot of a child's phone around a virtual map as the kid travels solo. I also know of at least one parent who justifies the smartphone for a boy with ADHD; the theory is that the more he uses his phone on the city bus the less likely he is to lose it, something he'd be likely to do with a phone that he used only occasionally for voice calls.

Everyone else, however, should consider the approach that Mary Kay Russell, the mother of four boys in Naperville, Illinois, has taken. The boys are welcome to have any smartphone they want whenever they have enough money to buy it. They also have to write a $360 check to their parents to cover the first year's data charges and continue paying for the service after that advance money has run out. The oldest boy waited until he was 21 to get a smartphone. A few strategies can help keep the cost low for first-time smartphone buyers paying out of a child-size budget. Consider used or refurbished phones. Check out a service like Ting, which can lower the monthly charges significantly by precisely itemizing the minutes and the data. And encourage the kids to try to access the Internet only via Wi-Fi, which is almost always available in many of the places where they spend time.

The Car: Whose Need, Really?

The smartphone judgment call is a mere warm-up for consideration of the automobile. Given the high price for even the least costly of vehicles, any discussion of the subject should begin with a handful of framing questions and policies. First comes the weighing of wants versus needs, but this time there's a twist: Sometimes it's the parent who feels the need for the child to have a car. If a newly licensed teenager is allowed, by law, to ferry younger siblings around, this end to parental chauffeuring can free an adult to work more hours, care for others, or enjoy some down time. In this case, it makes sense for the parents to pay.

Kids who work in a family business may be able to help a whole lot more if they have a car to drive too.

If a car is merely a want, then three issues arise: If a child is paying for all or part of it through a part-time job, there need to be some limits on the number of work hours, lest schoolwork suffer. Aside from the cost of the car itself, families have to decide who will pay for insurance, gas, and maintenance. Finally, it's a fine idea to have the kids research the vehicle options themselves, but minimum standards for safety equipment must apply.

Very quickly, it becomes clear how difficult it is for teenagers to pay all the costs associated with a car without spending every spare moment working to cover them. This probably isn't the result that most of us are seeking, so we're faced with three choices: Paying for a big chunk of this giant want, giving kids our old cars, or sharing our cars with them. One way to help make sure they contribute to the cost is by starting the car conversation at age 13 or so. If a child seems committed to car ownership, divert birthday and holiday gift budgets to a savings account for the vehicle. Consider matching the money teenagers are willing to save, which will give them all sorts of second thoughts about spending a cent of any money they make from part-time jobs. The money can always go toward college or other things later if they change their mind. Grandparents can help here too.

Hand-me-down cars may seem like elegant solutions. If there isn't any outstanding loan on the vehicle and plans are afoot to replace it anyway, it feels almost free for any family that manages to conveniently forget the lost trade-in value. Still, this is a big gift. If it's a want and not a need, consider assigning the child at least some financial responsibility for the ongoing maintenance, gas, or insurance costs.

The Fong family, who live outside Chicago, came up with an ingenious solution for their second car. Their son can use it almost any time, but they treat it like a Zipcar. He pays a monthly fee to help cover insurance. The rest is pay-as-you-go. That way, he has to think twice about the wisdom of driving to school when he can walk instead. Turns out he's not fond of having the car sit in the school lot racking up hourly fees all day.

Some of you are going to buy a new car for your child no matter what, and spring for gas and insurance as well. You can afford to splurge and do not see it as an indulgence if a child shows no emerging signs of entitlement. If that's the case, try at least to keep some of the allowance principles in mind. A child can certainly wait on the new automobile until several accident-free months have gone by in an older family car. An essay requirement might be in order, explaining what constitutes responsible use of the vehicle. And in that piece of writing, it might be wise to add a parental addendum explaining exactly what chores are mandatory for the gasoline to continue flowing.

Chores, Allowance, and Creative Kids

Many parents don't buy the idea that an allowance is practice money and that children should do chores for free. The American Institute of Certified Public Accountants ran a survey in 2012 that found that 89 percent of parents tied allowance to work around the house. The mutual fund company T. Rowe Price ran its own survey that same year and put the pay-for-chores figure at 86 percent. These parents believe that paying for work in the home is good training for the real world, where your compensation will depend on the timely and competent performance of assigned tasks. They also worry that if they simply hand out an allowance without asking anything in return, their kids will become lazy and entitled.

It's rare that anyone asks what the kids think about this question, but when they do, the replies are illuminating. The best example I could find is more than 100 years old, which just goes to show that the pay-for-chores debate is one that has vexed families for generations. In a collection of essays published in 1904, Blanche Dismorr used data she drew from essays written by British children of varying ages to write her own essay, "Ought Children to Be Paid for Domestic Services?" Among the 9-year-olds, 66 percent thought they deserved compensation for the work they do around the house. But just 36 percent of the 13-year-old children felt the same way. What changed in those four years of development? Dismorr pointed to two things—a growing awareness that everyone in the family ought to pitch in and a concern that demanding payment would make them selfish or mercenary.

While this study is practically ancient, the two rationales are timeless, and the kids are correct. If parents don't get paid for the regular work they do around the house, why should the kids? Chores are just something that everyone does to keep a household running. It's a fine idea for children to learn a proper work ethic, but parents can teach it by paying for larger, once-in-a-while tasks that they might otherwise hire someone else to do. And while we want our kids to know what it means to have a boss who evaluates their efforts, they are probably not going to end up working for their parents. So let them learn this from a real boss when they get jobs as teenagers, which they should definitely do.

As for the 13-year-olds who we fear will become mercenaries, think about how it could play out in our own homes. We may think we have some pull over our kids if chores are tied to an allowance. If they don't do the chores, after all, they won't get the money. But what happens if they decide they don't want or need the money? Chances are, we'll make them do the chores anyway. So why pay for them in the first place if these chores are ultimately mandatory in any event? There are plenty of other privileges we can withhold if kids aren't getting their chores done in a timely fashion. (Driving that new car, for instance.) Taking away money, which is a tool for learning, need not be one of them.

The only convincing counterargument I've heard on this topic comes from a San Francisco parent named Sotha Saing. Saing came to the United States as a Cambodian refugee in 1980 and started working in restaurants at the age of 12, earning money under the table. She spent any spare moments helping care for her autistic brother. After a brief period of homelessness, she eventually married and had four kids of her own. Today, they all live with her mother in a rental apartment in San Francisco, and Saing has a fledgling bookkeeping business.

Saing and her four children all save money through an organization called EARN, which matches the savings of low-income workers and their families in an attempt to help them improve their financial lot in life. When I tried my no-pay-for-chores logic out on her, she dismissed it as a rich person's conceit. "Give them allowance?" she said, raising her voice enough that the

other Starbucks patrons may have wondered if we were quarrel-
ing. "Why would you give them allowance? Because they're your
child? That's an entitlement issue there. Have they earned it?
Shown respect for it? Well, where does *your* money come from?
You and I both work for money, so why are my kids entitled to
my money? If I have to work, then they should feel like they have
to earn it too."

Her logic is powerful. If you can't shake the feeling that children should have to do something in exchange for an allowance,
there is a middle ground you might pursue. As a child, Seattle
copywriter Jake Johnson's parents paid him to do chores. But
when his 7-year-old son, Liam, started clamoring for a fourth
football and the latest Beyblades and a regular allowance to pay
for it all, Johnson stopped to consider what his own allowance
experience had taught him. Upon reflection, he decided that he
had learned two things: that he needed to rush to finish his everyday tasks so he could get paid and that working for money
was no fun at all.

What Johnson wanted for Liam, he wrote in an online essay that quickly went viral, was something different. He and his
wife hope that their son will learn to think entrepreneurially and
grow up to be someone who sells his ability to come up with creative ideas, not just his competence in performing tasks. They
want him to know that there can be joy in a job well done. So
while Liam earns no money for basic chores, he does get paid for
recognizing problems and solving them. When he spotted all the
fallen leaves in the backyard, he offered to rake them and nego-
tiated a price. His grandparents' dirty car inspired him to wash
it to make some money. Later he wanted to wash other people's

vehicles on a regular basis, and Jake helped him write a simple business plan. "I see passion building in him as he looks at making money as a project that involves solving problems rather than as selling his time to hurry through tasks," Jake wrote in his essay. "Every kid loves a good project, and so do I. I see him slowly turning into an entrepreneurial thinker. And no matter what he does in life, that type of thinking will help him excel."

4

The Smartest Ways for Kids to Spend

The hours-of-fun-per-dollar test,
Grandma Dana's shopping ritual, and the
importance of record-store pit stops

Back in high school, Annie Leonard was the kid without the Vuarnet sunglasses. One of three siblings, Leonard was raised by a single mother, a nurse; her mom had the wherewithal to get her into good private schools but not much spare money beyond that. Cars arrived at her high school on her classmates' 16th birthdays wrapped in pink ribbons, only to have grown-ups drive them away because students weren't supposed to have cars at school.

Leonard grew up to be an activist, traveling the globe for Greenpeace. Along the way, she made a short film about pollution and garbage called *The Story of Stuff* in hopes of teaching people about the consequences of buying and discarding more things than we truly need. It struck a nerve, a big one, and the video has now been viewed online at least 25 million times. The film became a book and evolved into a nonprofit organization. Stephen Colbert had her on his show and referred to her film as a "craze."

Children eventually joined the audience. Teachers began showing the film to classrooms full of students. Requests poured in for some sort of curriculum or lesson plan. A story about the film's popularity among educators appeared on the front page of *The New York Times*, complete with tales of children who were having second thoughts about their Lego purchases. All the attention among the juvenile set was surprising to Leonard, since it had never been the point of the exercise. "I didn't make *The Story of Stuff* for kids," she explained. I was surprised when she told me this, for she is a mother herself. But she eventually came to understand that one of the reasons she was able to explain the cycle of stuff so well is that she'd spent so many years trying to explain her work to her now teenage daughter, Dewi.

So how does a mother who takes a bold public stand against mindless buying go about raising a child in this day and age? Well, Leonard is no eco-scold in real life, and her parenting is a lot like mine or yours. She owns a car, and she and her neighbors share a trampoline and swimming pool, both firmly in the Wants category. Nor is she cheap. Dewi goes skiing and spends a fair bit of time at a local rock-climbing gym. And mother and daughter negotiate over skinny jeans and standards of appropriate attire the same way most of us do with our own kids.

We all have our own stories behind our collections of stuff and the feelings those possessions generate—pride of ownership in something we saved for long and hard, gratitude for an heirloom or a constant stream of hand-me-downs, bewilderment at the enormous assortment of outgrown sports gear that piles up, regret about things we barely use but cost enough to make us feel bad about putting them out on the curb. Given the sheer abundance of our modern lives, it's not surprising that we end up with so many complicated feelings and concerns about stuff. Never before has so much been available for so little with such ease, whether it's the fast fashion at H&M or the fast food at the chains that so many kids love. On the one hand, this is frightening. All of us remember the economic collapse in 2008, where many people spent and borrowed beyond their means. We want to train our kids somehow to resist such urges and protect them from the consequences of succumbing to them.

On the other hand, there is real joy in spending money on objects and experiences that bring lasting happiness and enduring memories. This pleasure is not something to be ashamed of or to chide our children for. In fact, we ought to celebrate it. The first time I watched my daughter buy something with her own money, she was shopping for jewelry at an outdoor festival and stalked the displays under the tent with such determination and pride, clenching the bills in her little fist. It was a real moment for her, and I'm sure there will be more of them as she saves up for bigger things. We shouldn't rob our kids of these pleasures.

What they need is a sense of balance and just the right amount of thrift. Thrift is an odd word, often synonymous with cheap. If it's ever a compliment, it's a begrudging one. What's been lost over the years, however, is the recognition that the root word of thrift is *thrive*. Our goal as parents isn't to promote the stingy type of thrift or the resolute version that previous generations of Americans generally turned to only when the economy or war shortages demanded it. Instead, we're aiming to do three things: set some spending guidelines to lean on; model a few sensible tactics for our children; and adopt family rituals that make spending fun—but only on things that have real value and meaning. With this foundation, we'll give our kids the best shot at thriving no matter how much money they end up having or what is going on with the economy.

The Fun Ratio and the More-Good/Less-Harm Rule

Start with one great calculation that kids can do as soon as they learn simple division. It comes from Mary Matthiesen, a scientist by training, who first posted about it in my Facebook community. Most kids go through an extended "I want, I want" stage. It's tiresome in and of itself, but it can be especially disappointing if you lack the proper comeback. "We can't afford it" isn't always true, and "because I said so" isn't particularly satisfying to anyone. Saying yes to preserve the peace doesn't feel so good either, given that kids often end up with toys or souvenirs that they don't play with much once they are cluttering up the house.

But Matthiesen hit on the concept of return on investment, though she didn't call it that. Instead, she asked her kids to estimate the hours of fun per dollar that any particular Want of theirs might provide. The idea came to her around Christmas. Her son's most expensive toys, a Talking Tigger and a Tekno Pup, grabbed his attention but didn't hold it for very long. Meanwhile, the cheapest toys, a Fisher-Price cash register and a Blue's Clues playhouse, entertained both kids for hours. The house eventually fell to pieces, while the cash register lasted for years. She did the math for me and crowned the cash register champion at 185.5 hours of fun per dollar, while Talking Tigger yielded just 0.08 hour of fun per dollar. The best deal, the kids realized years later, was a deck of cards. It lasts a lifetime as long as you don't lose any of them, and it doesn't cost more than $2 or so. She knew her daughter had gotten the concept when she walked through a toy store one day, hit Press Me on a talking doll, and quipped, "Well, I just got my five minutes of fun for free."

The kids are now 20 and 17 and the family lives in Lakewood, Ohio. Jimmy, the older one, eventually used the ratio to convince his parents to pay for some video games. Thousands of hours of fun for $60 is worth the expense, the logic went. He listens to music on Spotify now instead of buying it and tolerates the commercials on the free version. Most of the movies he sees he streams on Netflix; two hours of fun per dollar for 10 movies a month at $10 a month for the service. Sarah, the 17-year-old, reads a lot of library books and buys few books at the store. The library card costs nothing at all, whereas a $10 book might provide just 0.5 hours of fun per dollar for a fast reader who finishes it in five hours.

The Fun Ratio works particularly well for things we don't buy every day—the Wants more than the Needs. Those purchases tend to be the first ones that children are interested in making anyway, like toys. Later on, the whole family can do the math on experiences that the grown-ups may or may not be willing to pay for. The Fun Ratio helps, for instance, when setting budgets for vacations, which is a discussion that teenagers can participate in. It's useful when an event has already happened, too. Did everyone agree that the more expensive tickets to a concert or other event were worth it? What other fun might everyone have had with the savings from sitting in the cheaper seats?

When it comes to more everyday Needs, though—things like food or clothing—the Fun Ratio doesn't help quite as much. For those instances, I like the test that Zoe Weil came up with as part of her work as president of the Institute for Humane Education. In an effort to explain to students how she made her own consumer decisions, she told them that she asked herself a single question: Which one does the most good and the least harm?

The More-Good/Less-Harm Rule is not a new test. It's just an extension of the Golden Rule, a version of which turns up in the good and holy books of nearly every world religion. It's also highly flexible. More good and least harm for whom? You? Your neighbors? Your nation? The environment? Animals? The implicit but essential message here is that every dollar we spend is an endorsement of something. Which is not to say that we need to remind our children of this every time we buy something. That would be exhausting—and not just for the kids. Also, Weil freely acknowledges that we don't always have enough information to figure out what actually will help more and harm less.

Sometimes, however, there is plenty of information. Take the Abercrombie & Fitch chain of clothing stores for instance. It not only fired a teenage employee for wearing an Islamic headscarf, it went to federal court to defend its right to do so. It has sold shirts with sayings across the chest that read "Who Needs a Brain When You Have These?" and "Gentlemen Prefer Tig Ol' Bitties" and "Do I Make You Look Fat?" Over the years, its chief executive has defended its thong underwear for girls that had "Eye Candy" and "Wink Wink" printed on the front and proclaimed that "a lot of people don't belong [in our clothes], and they can't belong. Are we exclusionary? Absolutely." Many teens will find out about company behavior like this on their own and decide for themselves whether to patronize it. But parents can certainly direct kids' attention to questionable behavior in the service of asking what sort of harm they might cause by spending their dollars at a company that seems to be up to no good.

The same logic applies when making choices about where to spend money in the community. For children who play in the local Little League, ask them to think about which businesses gave money to sponsor the teams. Or maybe there were others that helped with the annual PTA auction. Perhaps you have a friend or neighbor who is a local merchant. Parents can go out of their way to spend money at these businesses and encourage kids to do the same with their allowance money.

Spending money at a local farmers market is another way to support people who live nearby. It seems obvious to grown-ups, but children have no way of knowing what spending money there accomplishes unless we explain it and remind them once in a while.

The Value of Coupons, Prepaid Debit Cards, and Thrift-Store Shopping

Once we've established some guidelines for spending, it's a good idea to introduce some tools to help kids spend their money more wisely and some new places where they can get more for every dollar.

Plenty of good comes from using coupons, and nobody is harmed in their use. So introducing kids to this practice as a way to get them to think about spending money wisely makes sense. Some veteran couponers bring their kids in on the weekly grocery store battle plan and turn it into a game with actual cash prizes that reflect the family's savings.

Each week, starting when she was about 7 years old, Katie Belpedio Schreiber, her mother, and her younger brother would sit down at the kitchen table with the *Columbus Dispatch* in Ohio, and clip. The coupons went in an accordion file that the trio would take to the local Kroger or Big Bear, depending on which had the best in-store deals that week. The children waited by the register for the receipt to announce the total savings, and their mother would hand it over on the spot, in cash. Each child usually got around $6 on a $100 grocery bill. Belpedio Schreiber no longer has to watch her pennies quite as carefully as her parents once did, but she still eagerly rips open the coupon mailers that come to her house.

Another tactic that encourages thrift, cuts down on endless nagging, and gives kids some sense of autonomy is the use of prepaid debit cards. These work particularly well during trips or in situations where parents are paying but want the kids to stick to a budget. Lori Embrey, a financial planner in Columbus, Ohio, wanted a ready answer for the chorus of "can I get this?" she feared she would hear on an endless loop when her family went to Disney World for a week. So each kid got a $100 prepaid card that they could use for anything beyond basic food and drinks, which were on Mom and Dad. She even devoted one piece of luggage to snacks and Ziploc bags, so they could choose to tote those around rather than paying $5 for Dippin' Dots and the like. The combination of a strictly finite resource and the control built into having a card of one's own practically forces a child to think about value and trade-offs. Still, it puts the kids in control, which makes them feel powerful. Even Embrey's 5-year-old son totally got it; he thought hard about his purchases and didn't pick his souvenirs until the last day of the trip. He also had enough left over for ice cream.

Cards that we designate for a specific purpose can be useful budgeting tools even when we're not on vacation or at an amusement park for the day. For instance, we can set up children who love games with a card loaded with a limited amount of allowance money for in-app purchases alone. Parents who want to pay for their kids to go off campus for lunch once a week during the school year can automatically transfer a set dollar amount to a card every month. In exchange for the privilege of going out, the child has to keep track of the card and its balance.

One great retail venue for instilling values about spending and saving is thrift shops. They're easy to find in most towns of any size, and kids often see going to them as the treasure hunts they often are. Aimee Sims has been shopping with her family at thrift shops for years. Her husband is in the military, so he's in uniform during the workday and doesn't need a large wardrobe. When he was deployed in conflict zones overseas, he earned hazard pay, as did many of his fellow soldiers whose families lived on base back in the United States. Aimee saw their spouses spending this extra money on boats and other luxuries, but she decided to use it to pay off the family's vehicle loans and funnel the rest toward chasing $5 cashmere sweaters in second-hand stores. The family lives in northern Virginia now, and Aimee's daughter has grown to see the advantages of shopping at thrift stores. "The fashion now is skinny jeans with a hoodie sweatshirt and some kind of funny T-shirt," Aimee said, describing

the teenagers she sees parading around. Her daughter has realized that not only are the funny T-shirts often just $1 in thrift
shops, but nobody else will ever have the same one. She loves the
pursuit and takes pride in her ability to outsmart the commercial marketplace.

Family Rituals: Dollar-Store Dana, Record-Store Pit Stops, and the Teachings of Lent

One of my favorite ways to set family values into place is to build
rituals around certain kinds of spending. While parents should
take the lead, there's a grandmother in Chicago who started a
family tradition worthy of copying, particularly for parents of
smaller children. Every year on the birthdays of her three grandchildren, Dana Treister handed each of them a dollar for every
year they'd been alive. Then, she took them to a dollar store so
they could pick out gifts for themselves. With a small pile of dollars, everything in a true, old-fashioned dollar store is, by definition, affordable. So figuring out what to buy becomes a great
way to test how well your children are absorbing the lessons
you're trying to teach.

Grandma Dana started her dollar-store trips when each of
her grandchildren turned 4. One key, she explained, was never
having a time limit so the kids could carefully weigh their
choices. Some dollar-store trips would take 90 minutes. One of
her grandchildren would walk the aisles methodically, another
would grab everything interesting and then put things back
at the end. The third grandchild, on one of her first birthday

visits, picked out a dog Frisbee. Grandma Dana had to probe her a bit on this, given that the intended recipient was an old and lethargic pug. Would Harley really run after the spinning disk? Was the dog's mouth big enough to catch a Frisbee in the first place? They soon determined that the dog would get many more hours of fun out of a stuffed pink bone. This tradition went on for nearly a decade, until the older kids grew out of the selection of toys but hadn't yet learned to appreciate the bargains on cleaning products.

My colleague Dwight Garner and his wife, Cree LeFavour, adopted a family buying ritual years ago with their two children. Whenever they see an independent record store, they stop and buy something. "Record stores tend to be great places," Garner explained. "Cluttered and alive and pretty weird. Good places for kids to see. Walking around record stores with them helps teach the lesson that selling their music is how musicians make a living. It's not OK to rip your music from illegal sites."

This rule is thick with values and virtues. It instills the habit of seeking out novelty and adventure as a family. It teaches the importance of neighborhood shops and the people who work in them, reverence for the artists who enrich our lives, and the value of fair play and honest dealings. And when grown-ups find the perfect recording of a favorite record from long ago for far less money than they might have imagined, the lasting joy and power of that discovery and the possibility of finding more like it calls to mind the Fun Ratio.

There are so many other ritualistic experiences that inspire similar passion and deliver cheap thrills. Visiting garage sales? Riding all the best roller coasters? My family makes a point of seeking out local ice cream shops as much as possible while traveling. We also dutifully sample every new flavor that manages to get into our local grocer's freezer and subscribe to a monthly ice cream delivery service where the mad scientist chefs whip up flavors such as smoked hay or candy corn or frozen essence of mango sticky rice. In the summer, we also stop at any stand where kids are selling lemonade or crafts or other things. We always ask what they are going to do with the money, and there's often a great story that they're eager to share.

The rituals need not all be around spending. Every so often, it's useful to introduce the idea of organized restraint. Joshua Yates picked some of this idea up as a middle schooler, when he worked in his family's cherry orchard in Bigfork, Montana. His mother, Cynthia Yates, wrote personal finance books, including *1,001 Bright Ideas to Stretch Your Dollars* and *The Complete Guide to Creative Gift-Giving*. When he was in eighth grade, she gave him a keychain for his birthday with a quote on it that said, "God first, others second, you last." This sort of sacrifice is a lot to ask of a child, but the memory stuck with him, as it reinforced his family's generous, principled nature.

Yates grew up to be a sociology professor, and he and a colleague eventually assembled a book-length collection of essays from other academics about the history and idea of thrift. Part of what he discovered is that any vision for thrift in a particular era almost inevitably became something that grown-up authority figures lectured about to kids. But as the father of four in Charlottesville, Virginia, he and his wife now realize that they shouldn't count on anyone else to define thrift and thriving for them. Politicians don't talk much about individual thrift anymore, even if they do complain about governmental bloat. Schools no longer teach the concept much either, except as a quirky footnote to American history. "Ultimately, it has to be part of the narrative of our own family identity, that this is what living well will mean," he said. "Our kids are going to have to navigate this on their own at some point. And the point isn't to become a simple lifer and check out and try to buy a farm and go off the grid. I grew up in Montana so I know people who have done that!"

So they watch *The Christmas Carol* as a family and talk about the lessons of the film. They recently pulled over while on a road trip to purchase lottery tickets for everyone and talked about how the game works and the long odds but also fantasized at length about how they'd all choose to spend the winnings. At home, Yates finds himself repeating something his father used to say, which is that their house is not a resort but a homestead. They all pitch in, and no one gets an allowance for doing regular chores. Yates got his first Sony Walkman as a sort of wage in exchange for work on the family cherry orchard; his kids pay for iPods by doing additional one-off jobs in return for money.

And once in a while, often during Lent or Advent, they'll give up something for a bit as a family. It's not because the parents disapprove of material objects or don't want their kids craving things and saving up for them; it's just to reinforce the idea that it's also possible to take a break from them and acknowledge that so many of these things are merely wants and not needs. "It teaches the kids, as it does me, that these goods are here to serve us, and it's not us who serve them," he said. "There are so few opportunities to rest. You have to have some ways of building them in."

To Yates, this is part of an ongoing effort to give his children the power to say no to things in the precious few years that they are watching what their parents do and absorbing what they say. It's a noble goal that we all should share, but it's also wise to be realistic about how much impact our example and our words can have on our kids. Even if it's easier to keep them away from television commercials than it used to be, their peers and strangers they encounter have spending habits that broadcast messages of their own.

Creating Your Own Counterprogramming

As Annie Leonard contemplated her own relationship with stuff and how she wanted to try to shape her daughter Dewi's attitude about what to spend and why, she kept returning to Boston University psychologist Juliet Schor's explanation of outside influence and its effect on the way we spend money. Schor refers to these influences as our vertically expanded reference groups. In the old days, we'd compare our furniture or clothes or car horizontally with our neighbors', who were often a lot like us. Today, our point of reference has grown vertically—mostly up—since we're now able to see the inside of celebrities' closets on reality shows and track their day-to-day outfits on a thousand different websites and apps. "For years, every time I went to New York City, I bought a pair of shoes," Leonard said. "Once I learned about this phenomenon, I could go to New York, see all the amazing shoes and resist the urge to buy by saying, 'oh, it's the vertical expansion of my reference group. In three days I'll be back home in Berkeley where everyone is wearing clogs.'"

Older children's reference groups have gone vertical as well, on all forms of social media. One of the purest expressions of this is the phenomenon of the "haul" video. In these online clips, teens empty the contents of their enormous shopping bags from fast fashion stores like Zara and Forever 21 and then offer up commentary on what they bought and why. Some of the most popular haulers, like Blair Fowler, who started shooting the selfie videos when she was a teenager in Tennessee, draw more than one million views per clip—enough so that they've heard from haters who accuse them of boasting. Fowler makes a point in one video of saying that she works two part-time jobs to save money for beauty products and clothes. It's but a short moment, however, in a 10-minute explanation of six-dollar denim day (when jeans are marked down to that price) and other retail phenomena. She can't even determine the color of one of the skirts she just bought but remembers that a friend who shopped with her told her it would look great with a fun pair of tights.

It's against this backdrop, which normalizes the idea of teens buying loads of clothes by literally making a show of it, that Annie Leonard offers her own counterprogramming. She doesn't set the DVR to avoid commercials on her television. Instead, she turns the reading of commercial messages into a game with her daughter. "We have a race to see who can say first what subliminal messages they're trying to send us," she said.

When I showed my own daughter a haul video for the first time she quickly said, "That's bragging." I hope she continues to feel that way when she gets more access to online media, but it will probably be challenging. Still, talking regularly to our kids about how others talk about the things they've bought allows us to remind them why our own families spend money the way we do.

When Annie Leonard became executive director of Green-peace USA not so long ago, she did not immediately sell her car or drain the pool that she shares with the neighbors. The pool is one of those solo operations where you swim against an artificial current to simulate laps, and it embarrasses her a little. "When we were getting it, I said, 'We can just go over to the YMCA to swim,'" she recalled. "But the truth is, it's great. Everyone swims so much more."

Still, the sharing itself is a symbol of one of her own family's rules for thrift and thriving: the idea that there are things we can borrow instead of buy, which frees up money for purchasing the things and experiences that deliver the most joy and the strongest memories. Leonard loves Granny Smith apples, and some of her other neighbors have trees. In the autumn, she often comes home to a bag of apples by her front door. An e-mail she sent to a wider circle of neighbors when her daughter was interested in learning to ski didn't yield scolding replies about the environmental hazards of snowmaking equipment or the gas necessary to drive to the mountain. Instead, people dropped off bags of outgrown boots and clothing within 24 hours. "My daughter has learned that when we have a need, we first turn to the community," she said. "This is liberating financially. It's made us able to do more things than we could have otherwise."

Sometimes, however, the effort can go too far. For the first 10 years of her life, Leonard's daughter was fine with the hand-me-downs that they picked up at a cousin's house and stored in their garage. Then, when she was in fourth grade, Dewi approached her mother with a request. "I have to tell you something that might disappoint you," she told her mother. "I'd like to go clothes

shopping." Her mother, who laughs about the story now, reminded her how many clothes she already had, but her daughter would not be swayed. "I know, but the only place we ever go
shopping is the garage," she said, laughing at her own joke.

She wanted skinny jeans. From Old Navy—where the clothes
don't last long and come from the kinds of factories that her
mother criticized in *The Story of Stuff* and that she worries
about at Greenpeace. But Leonard bit her tongue and took her
shopping there. No brands are banned in Leonard's home. Dewi
is not expressly forbidden to spend money on clothes made in
Bangladesh or other countries where factory owners have mis-
treated workers. Leonard merely asks her to consider these issues, respect her body, be smart and safe, and then make up her
own mind.

"She has to learn and develop her own sense of values herself," she said.

5

Are We Raising Materialistic Kids?

*The tooth fairy, the travel-team dilemma,
and the making of a more modest school*

The father of Bramson Dewey worked 80 to 90 hours a week for his entire adult life at his tiny wholesale company. It was one of those anonymous businesses you never hear much about, distributing goods from manufacturers to stores. The Dewey business had been around long enough that it once used horses and buggies, and it had operated out of two different storefronts in Chicago.

On Sunday Bramson's father, Mike, rested but he didn't let up. If his wife had spent $1.29 instead of $1.09 for two liters of soda, it could send him into a rage that lasted for days. Bramson spent years waiting to join the local youth sports leagues because Mike didn't see the point of letting his son play and paying the fees it would require. Another family took Bramson to buy used hockey equipment with money he'd earned working, since Mike wasn't about to pay for any gear.

Bramson and his brother were the kids who didn't go to restaurants, have Atari, or go away on family vacations. They never asked why and didn't stop to wonder whether their family was struggling financially or whether their father was just trying to teach them something. "He never spoke to any of us any more than to maybe tell us something he wanted done," Bramson explained. "There were no life lessons or guidance of any kind."

Bramson did pick up a pretty good work ethic, though. He delivered newspapers as a kid, cleared dirty dishes at a country club while in high school, and loaded trucks for a moving company when he was in college. As a young adult, he became an accountant, a white-collar job with a series of increasingly prestigious titles with each promotion.

His skill with numbers ended up being quite useful to his family in a way he could never have expected. In 2001 his father was diagnosed with cancer, and somebody had to help him keep the business running while he received treatment. Bramson's mother, who had never so much as written a check, played courier and ferried brown paper bags filled with cash and paperwork to the hospital so Bramson could help run his father's company from there. "It was like a forensic audit for me to figure out which way was up and everything that was going on," he recalled.

Bramson's heavily medicated father slipped in and out of consciousness, but when he was lucid, Mike realized he had no choice but to answer at least some of his son's questions. And slowly, as Mike revealed as little as he needed to and Bramson opened his mail, it dawned on Bramson that the state of his father's business was not quite what he had thought. There was the $500,000, for instance, that had been sitting in a checking account for who knows how long, earning nothing.

When Bramson found no mortgage bills, things began to click into place. His father owned the side-by-side buildings where his business was headquartered, including all the apartments up above. And when he'd moved the business into these buildings in 1968, he'd held on to the previous building, which had its own set of apartments. When he started doing the math, he realized that his father was worth millions of dollars and that the apartment rents alone brought in six figures each year.

Mike died within a year, and Bramson, his brother, and his mother inherited the buildings. They shut down the wholesale business, spruced up the properties, and hired a management company to handle day-to-day building matters. The rents they were collecting grew so high that Bramson himself was eventually able to quit working as an accountant. At the age of 36, he became a stay-at-home parent.

Given his family history, he could easily have made any number of mistakes with his two daughters. Often, people whose own mother and father refused to spend much money have trouble ever saying no to their children when they become parents. Their own memories of constantly hearing no and doing without are painful, especially if their own parents could have provided so much more but simply chose not to.

But the question of what kind of parent Bramson was going to be is just an outsize version of the one that many parents face: How do we strike the right balance between modesty, which in this context is all about restraint, and materialism?

Full Provisioning: A New Normal
for Kids and Consumerism

Every new generation of parents is astounded and somewhat alarmed when confronting the goods and experiences available to their children. But there's something about the always-on, instant-access, no-waiting nature of so much of life in recent years that really does seem fundamentally different.

Everyday luxury has become the new normal during our own adult lives. The Drybar blow-out salons for women, the handbag maker Coach (once fancy and now mainstream), and even Starbucks are part of this phenomenon, one that barely existed when many of us were children. The Stanford expert on adolescence, William Damon, writes matter-of-factly of the many children "who have privileges that were once reserved for royalty." And Tim Kasser, one of the leading experts on materialism among the nation's academic psychologists, reminds his readers how easy it is to forget that much of the world has never had a hot shower.

Like many of you, I imagine, I remember what a big deal it was for anyone to get a television in their bedroom as a teenager and the aching my friends and I all had for a private phone line. And who can forget the first family in the neighborhood to have a Betamax video tape player or a personal computer with a modem? Given how special these acquisitions were at the time, it seems somehow insane to hand every sixth grader a go-anywhere private line that's also a Handycam, Walkman, Swatch, VCR, Kodak Instamatic, pager, and book. Sure, it's miraculous and wonderful that a device that does all these things costs much less than the combined price of all of those other items 20 or 30 years ago. But it also goes to show just how much our baselines have changed.

So how do parents begin to define what constitutes an appropriate number of possessions and experiences? We all want to make up our own minds and do what feels right, but everything we do happens against a backdrop of whatever is going on in our particular communities. Allison J. Pugh, now a sociology professor at the University of Virginia, spent a couple of years following both affluent and struggling families around Oakland, California, and described them in a book called *Longing and Belonging*. What she determined is that our children are constantly navigating something she refers to as an "economy of dignity." In doing so, their feelings of self-worth often rise or fall depending on constantly shifting standards around the possessions and experiences that matter in their own little worlds.

Pugh, who saw these economies playing out in both poor and affluent communities, starkly describes the feelings that many children experience when they don't have a Game Boy or haven't been to the vacation destinations that most of the other kids are talking about. For kids with nothing to contribute and no bragging rights, it's akin to "a sort of unwelcome invisibility." Pugh describes the "matching" that goes on when they make meek attempts to interject with information about a different (cheaper) game or other (closer) destination that's barely relevant. Kids want to belong, so this is one way of saving face. Perhaps unsurprisingly, the privileged among them engage in what Pugh refers to as "patrolling," sniffing around the dignity claims of others in order to pass judgment. They run, she concludes, a "dignity gauntlet." In this sort of environment, many parents attempt to shield their kids from any psychic blows by providing a "full provisioning" that leaves them wanting for practically nothing.

How Materialistic Kids Are Made

That full kit of toys and clothes and gear and enrichment does not make every kid into an overindulged problem child. So how do you know one when you see one—or are in danger of accidentally raising one? Social scientists have spent decades weighing in on this: Materialistic people focus more on stuff than they do on people and relationships. (On a playdate, this looks like a persistent inability to share the object of greatest desire in the room.) They genuinely believe that more stuff will make them happy. (Whining and begging unrelentingly even after they're out of preschool and ought to be able to accept no for an answer.) They care less about the utility of their stuff and more about what sort of reaction people will have to it. (Bragging after parents capitulate in the face of their begging.) They want too much of the wrong things, or they want their things in the wrong way. (More things than they need without having to pay for them with allowance money or to wait for them.) And the fallout is unpleasant in countries all over the world; multiple studies have shown that materialism is correlated with higher levels of depression and anxiety and a range of ills from backaches to drug use.

We want to deploy whatever tactics we can to keep kids from becoming materialistic, so let's call out one obvious bogeyman:

Children who watch lots of television commercials are clearly vulnerable. Yes, they take in all sorts of commercial messages each day whether we want them to or not. But given how easy it is to keep them away from many direct pitches when they're still too young to decode (and mock) the salesmanship, why wouldn't we? One of the most eye-opening studies in this realm involved a bunch of 4- and 5-year-olds who watched a commercial for something called the Ruckus Rangers, while the control group did not. Of those who didn't see the commercial, 70 percent wanted to play in a sandbox with friends instead of playing with the toy, while only 36 percent of the kids who saw the commercial chose friends over the Rangers.

Then came the follow-up: Given the choice between playing with a nice boy who didn't have any Ruckus Rangers and a not-so-nice boy who did, just 35 percent of the kids who had seen the commercial chose to hang out with the nice boy with no toy. When researchers asked the same question the next day, it had gone up but only to 49 percent. The commercials actually seem to have caused the kids to value getting their hands on the toy over the virtues of their playmate. As for the kids who hadn't seen the commercial, 70 percent chose the nice boy to play with.

So set the DVR or download entertainment that comes free of commercials. That's the easy part. The rest involves reckoning with our own impact on our kids. It begins with the example we set when we spend on ourselves. After I spoke at a school several years ago, a mother came up to me afterward and asked me a question very quietly. What should she tell her daughter who wanted to know why she can't show horses given that her father drives a luxury car?

I laughed at the time, and so did the mother; it's easy to dismiss this as a bad case of teenage entitlement. But remember, it's their job to ask questions, even presumptuous ones rooted in outsize expectations. Most of us will eventually be in the position where they'll ask us to explain our own large purchases or extravagances. What will we say? Is every car or handbag or vacation defensible? And what does it mean if we feel defensive about it? Can we explain it all without scolding the child who is asking what is, at its root, a reasonable question, even if the tone of voice is a little bratty? After all, they just want to know what we stand for; our spending choices is one way that we articulate this.

Bold questions like this also result from pent-up frustration. We control so much, and they know it. Kids run the dignity gauntlet in outfits and arenas that are mostly of our choosing, not theirs. We decide what they can wear, what they can have, where they live and go to school, and what they can do when they're not in class. Setting strict limits on all of this seems like the right default, even if we do drive nice cars ourselves. When we see them appearing literally to ache for things that other kids have or do, however, it often calls to mind our own feelings of childhood longing. And satisfying our kids' desire for dignity and a sense of inclusion in the present can make us feel like good parents, and signal to ourselves and the world that we are doing just fine. Dignity, it turns out, involves intense feelings for both parents and kids. So in practice, the quest for dignity usually involves kids nagging parents, offering questionable data about who has or does what, and in what quantity.

But sometimes, the desire to do what everyone else does—and to provide what everyone else provides—is a parental affliction alone. Consider the scenes that unfold at some overnight camps during visiting day each summer. Frantic families queue up well before the appointed hour. So desperate are they to get to their kids and deliver all manner of goodies unto them that at least one camp sets up a rope line to hold the grown-ups back, as if it were a presidential visit where strict security is necessary. After a chanted countdown, with families shouting "10, 9, 8 . . ." at the top of their lungs, counselors drop the rope and the parents take off running, shouting instructions to drop the blankets on a prime patch of grass or to secure the best spot on the tiny beach fronting the lake.

Parents bring towers of candy so large that they need shopping carts and wagons to transport them. Comments on a clip from a visiting-day video that went viral tell of one family that brought a generator to power the microwave to pop a child's favorite popcorn. Another copped to having turned up with a full spread from Chipotle, complete with portable buffet tables, chafing dishes, and Sterno cans. They set it all up under a large covered tent that they had toted along, just in case it rained. Moms and dads worried about food allergies bring custom sweatshirts or custom socks for the whole cabin in lieu of treats. Others set out a spread for their own kid and buy "bunk gifts" for everyone in their child's cabin as well.

This orgy of immodesty goes far beyond the mere maintenance of any one camper's dignity. But parents who send their kids to camps like this without having realized how high the visiting-day stakes are insist that you make the mistake of coming late or empty-handed only once. Besides, it's about love, they say, not materialism. To which I say: If these are the kinds of things we talk *ourselves* into doing for our kids, there's no telling what our children's powers of persuasion can accomplish.

Our temptation to indulge or loosen the rules is also an opportunity to rethink the role of peer pressure, a phrase that many of us use without realizing it usually doesn't begin with children. If kids lose face because others have toys or experiences that they do not, it's only because their friends' parents let them have that stuff and do those things in the first place. The same is true with late curfews or the freedom to go anywhere after school. Or being allowed to forgo chores or avoid other contributions to the family.

Sure, we can always say no. Many of us wish we could (or is it *would?*) a bit more often. No to the running on visiting day, no to the double piercing or tattoos, no to the newest phone and the latest inappropriate pop singer. But to take such a stand isn't just disappointing to our children. Other parents inevitably hear about it, and some of them surely interpret our own lines in the sand as a kind of silent (yet still somehow quite loud) judgment on the rules and choices they make for their own children. Unless, that is, we just go along to get along, which is easy to do when our kids want us to do that in the first place.

Antimaterialist Ideas from the
Professor of Materialism

When I began my quest to create a cradle-to-18 guide to keeping materialism at bay, it didn't take long to find the work of Tim Kasser. A psychology professor at Knox College in rural, west-central Illinois, he's the author of a book called *The High Price of Materialism*. He's also the father of two sons, so I asked him what parenting tactics he'd deployed to discourage materialism in his family.

His conclusions about materialism's high cost was not one he came to after a miserable upbringing. His childhood in Florida was perfectly pleasant and included plenty of video games and television. His father, who jokes that he's the model for his son's research, moved the family to a bigger house in a better neighborhood when Kasser was a teen.

He used his college years to question everything but not because he aimed to reject anything his family stood for. Instead, he was curious about how different people construct their lives and set goals. In graduate school, he noticed that there wasn't much research on the content of people's goals and one day wondered, almost on a lark, whether people who said that money was an important part of their goals were less happy. Back then, you had to wait a few minutes for a computer to analyze a data set, but after a bit of time ticked by, he got the result: There was indeed a correlation. He found this fascinating, kept replicating the results, and decided to make the study of materialism part of his life's work.

And then, like Bramson Dewey, he became a certain kind of parent—one with especially unusual experience and knowledge that was more or less destined to be part of his child-rearing philosophy. Today, his boys are teenagers and, unsurprisingly, neither of them is particularly materialistic. They live 8 miles south of Galesburg, Illinois, in a small, economically diverse town called Knoxville. The Kassers may have more money than many others in town, but their neighbors don't necessarily know it. The family prioritizes spending on travel and other experiences over the kinds of possessions that people might notice.

Until the boys were about 10, they could watch half an hour of television each day, as long as it was commercial-free, but the parents didn't keep a stopwatch running and movie-viewing didn't necessarily count against the next days' allotment of screen time. The rules went out the window when the family was staying at a hotel, however, and the boys' grandparents blew the rules off entirely, as grandparents often do. The boys eventually lobbied successfully for an increase to 45 minutes when they started playing video games, albeit ones prescreened by their parents.

Two years ago, their parents tried an experiment that many of us might want to emulate if we have the guts: They removed all of those time limits. The idea was that it was probably best for the boys to learn to regulate themselves while still under their parents' watchful eyes and that these self-regulatory skills would help them with budgeting of all sorts, including money. "You should have seen the looks on their faces when we decided this," Kasser recalled. Still, the boys knew the experiment would end if things got out of hand, so they set a timer themselves. Today, they no longer use it but still limit their game playing to that same 45 minutes give or take. "One of the best moments of my life as a parent was when my older son and I were sitting in the living room, and he thanked me for putting limits on his playing because so many of his friends were addicted to video games," he said.

The family does not avoid TV ads entirely, and sometimes they watch them for sport, as we all should once in a while. For many years, they would page through *National Geographic*, where all ads are at the front or the back, pointing them out. Kasser took great delight when one of his sons, at the age of 18 months, managed to parrot the phrase "They want my money!" back at his parents. When the family was traveling together, they would mute the hotel television during commercials and play what became a favorite game. Kasser would make up absurd fake dialogue that made fun of whatever the ad was trying to sell, and eventually the kids started doing it too. "My kids are going to be exposed to this stuff," he said. "So they need to know how to interact with it, and I tried to give them a different attitude about it."

The family is also big on giving custom coupons in lieu of gifts. When the boys were younger, there were ones for extra screen time or skipping the vegetable and still getting dessert. One favorite was the drop-everything-and-play-a-game-with-me-now coupon. The boys soon began returning the favor, offering a make-a-dessert coupon or one for mowing the lawn. Kasser remembers his father occasionally cutting out of work for an adventure with his kids, and now that his sons are older he offers special-day coupons to them. Early on, this might have involved going to the donut shop and playing chess. More recently, it's included Blue Man Group tickets and a trip to Peoria for one son's first meal in a fancy restaurant. "Plenty of times it would be a lot easier and cheaper to give them something," Kasser said. But his own memories of doing this with his dad are strong enough that he believes it's worth doing something unique with each boy when he can.

This doesn't mean that Kasser and his wife are hammering away on their boys about the evils of commercialism. There are no dinner-table lectures warning them away from caring too much about buying things or wanting to earn more than their father and mother, who is a counseling psychologist. "I don't want to make them into me," he said. "If my kids want to choose a career that is relatively ambitious in terms of the amount of work it will take and money they will make, well, it's not my life. You're there to love them and help pick up the pieces afterward if you need to."

Lost Teeth and Birthdays:
More Modest (but More Special)

Children love special events, and we love to celebrate with them. So how do we make these times unique and memorable without making them incredibly extravagant? The occasion of the first lost tooth is one great place to start, since kids often anticipate it for even longer than they look forward to each birthday or the arrival of Santa Claus. It's also one of the first occasions that specifically involves plain old cash.

Insurance provider Delta Dental puts out poll numbers each year on the going rate for a tooth. The most recent numbers put the price of a first tooth at $3.49 and the average price at $2.42. That's up 15 percent from the previous year. Very little else in the world gets more expensive at that pace, and if you need any proof of our default toward the full provisioning that Allison Pugh described, now you have it; in what is often our very first cash transaction with our children, we simply cannot keep the spending in check. Visa created an app to help parents see what the going rate was in their area (so they could exceed it, presumably). Dan Kadlec, who writes about personal finance for *Time*, declared the rising handout a bubble, akin to housing prices in 2005.

My wife and I had not prepared for this moment in our financial lives, so we turned to Facebook for advice when our daughter went to bed one night with a new gap in her smile. Within a couple of hours, several dozen responses poured onto my page. A former neighbor noted with some alarm that the going rate in the tonier parts of New York's Westchester County was $50 for the first tooth and $10 for subsequent teeth. An old basketball teammate of mine suggested $10 but added that he was from the North Shore, the Westchester County of Chicago. Plenty of others demanded that we give out the same $1 bill that we all got as kids. Fellow third-floor residents of our building noted that all the kids talk, and word was out about the neighborhood boy who got $20. They had told their son that there are different fairies on different blocks and suggested we give $5 just as they did so we could keep the ruse going.

My wife and I were most taken with the creative solutions: messages from the tooth fairy demanding improved dental hygiene; money obscured by a wrapping of minty dental floss; a fairy dust trail leading to the window; gold-colored dollar coins. We settled on the dust and the coins; the vending machine in our subway station gives change in $1 coins, and our daughter had never seen them before so they felt like treasure to her.

Later on, we heard two ideas that were even better. Bruce Feiler in *The New York Times* wrote about his disgust over the monetary imperative. Why should kids be rewarded for matters of biology? Still, he appreciated the fact that this was an opportunity to inject some magic into his twin daughters' lives just as they were growing out of the fairy stage. So when the first kid lost her first tooth, she was given a book called *Throw Your Tooth on the Roof,* which is about lost tooth traditions in other countries. Feiler and his wife also vowed to hand over coins in other currencies for each tooth, just to reinforce the idea of imagining life in other places.

Meanwhile, our friends Pam Briskman and Randy Weiner, lifelong educators and entrepreneurs, give out teeth from different animals when their daughters lose their own. So far, the lineup has included shark, coyote, lion, sheep, alligator, and rattlesnake—usually in glass jars filled with pink-colored water and glitter. The prize is accompanied by a note written backward so they have to hold it up to a mirror to read it, and it gives clues as to which animal the tooth once belonged to. They buy the teeth from a store in Albany, California, called the Bone Room. (It takes phone orders, in case you want to swipe the idea.)

This is a template for parental modesty—and parental awesomeness—that you can call on for birthday parties and vacations and any number of other situations where spending more money seems like the easiest way to keep your kids from feeling excluded from the conversation. As Weiner explained when describing the tooth fairy approach in his family, it's not the thing itself—the animal teeth—that's important. Instead, it's the values and intentions behind the thing. Their message is that they honor the rituals that their daughters hear about in school. But rather than doing it like everyone else, they're going to come up with a unique approach that will still give them something special to talk about if they want to.

When my wife and I were planning a slumber party with our about-to-be-8-year-old daughter, I suggested we used a Web service called ECHOage to handle invitations and gifts. When parents RSVP, they simply give ECHOage whatever money they would otherwise have spent on a gift. The service takes a small cut and then splits the rest. One half goes to a charity of the child's choosing, with the giver getting a tax deduction for that portion of the gift. The other half of the money goes straight to the child to buy one special gift instead of getting a bunch of smaller ones. This all seemed great in theory, as our daughter would be giving up half her presents, in effect, to a cause she cared about. On the surface, it seemed like a neat 50 percent reduction in materialism, and we'd be sparing guests having to shop for a gift.

Like many experiments, however, this one had a number of surprise outcomes. I hadn't counted on being able to see how much money the other parents were giving, but this information ended up being unavoidably apparent on the website. I genuinely didn't care or want to know. Once I saw that a few people had given $40 or $50, however, my mind filled with questions. Had people been generous because there were just a handful of girls coming who were our daughter's closest friends, so they wanted to spend a bit more on her? Or had they figured out that we would see what they gave and didn't want to appear cheap? Sure, they may have been moved by the concept and more generous for that reason alone. But perhaps they figured they should spend twice what they normally do so that neither the charity nor our daughter's gift got slighted somehow. The net result of our attempt to reduce birthday materialism a bit was that some people spent more money, not less. That felt odd, but my daughter was thrilled with the more expensive item she was able to buy and didn't miss the wrapping paper or small doodads she might have gotten otherwise.

We might all have more success conducting these sorts of experiments in our own immediate families around year-end holidays. Then, at least, we can control our own buying. Good luck, however, getting the grandparents to go along. They can be a menace in this regard, feeling as if it's their duty to eyeball whatever limits we try to set and obliterate them, especially come December. I say let them, as long as they're not undermining us on a regular basis. In fact, their generosity around the holidays can give us cover for making our own gifts more about charity, or taking a trip in lieu of token presents, or giving coupons like the Kassers, or doing something else that is entirely unique to each of us.

Travel Teams: The More We Spend, the More Pressure Kids Feel

One of the fastest-growing line items in family budgets is youth sports. Coaches encourage kids to train year-round and specialize at younger and younger ages. They succeed in part by holding out the possibility of a college scholarship or a boost in admissions odds to parents as an incentive for spending ever more money on one-on-one training and weekend travel for competitions. Some families love the road trips and togetherness, and the parents make enough money to foot the hotel bills comfortably.

But an increasing number are wondering whether they're being bamboozled into underwriting an entirely new form of overindulgence, particularly if the kids aren't having as much fun playing as they once did.

Travis Dorsch grew up to be a National Football League punter without any such pressure. He even played a second sport, baseball, in college at Purdue, and he had several more sports on his schedule throughout high school in Montana. He has fond memories of his parents coming to every single one of his college football games, and they seemed to know just what to do to make their presence feel supportive rather than burdensome. As a college senior, he discovered sports psychology and returned to Purdue when his football days were over to earn a PhD in the subject. He received his doctorate in 2013 and is now a rising star in his field due to his focus on the impact of youth sports on family life.

Dorsch's best-known research found that the more families spend on their children's participation in sports as a percentage of their income, the more likely children are to perceive pressure coming from their parents. And when they feel that pressure, they enjoy their sport less and are less likely to be motivated to continue. "I think parents find themselves out front pulling their kids in a certain direction," he said. "I try to teach parents what it means to be a supportive pusher and to stand behind their kids when they meet resistance."

Dorsch, who became a father himself in 2014, doesn't want parents to stop spending money on their children's athletic pursuits. Nor is he trying to convince them that their participation is somehow bad. But he does want all of us to have many more conversations with our kids about their goals and how much they want us looking over their shoulders. "Parents, especially of elite athletes, need to focus on how their kids are perceiving their involvement," he said. This can be as simple as asking them about it and having a frank conversation. It's fine to talk about the financial investment here as long as it's couched in supportive terms. "We're happy to spend this money on something you love as long as you're having fun and it makes you feel good about yourself," you might say. "But we also want you to know that you shouldn't do this to try to please us or because you think we expect you to win scholarship money, and we won't consider what we spent so far a waste if you decide that it's just not for you anymore." This could provide a strong sense of relief, just so long as it's true.

One School's Turn Toward More Modesty

When Mark Stanek, head of school at Shady Hill School, a pre-kindergarten-through-eighth-grade school in Cambridge, Massachusetts, took the job he decided to be honest with himself and the school community about its shifting demographics. Tuition had grown faster than inflation. Middle-class incomes had been stagnating for many years. Upper-middle-class families who lost jobs or saw their net worth fall or were simply scared out of their minds by the economic downturn stopped applying. Private schools like his had increasingly come to be populated by larger numbers of families who occupied a new stratosphere of wealth—ones who could pay the bills easily—and a smaller group of families who split a few million dollars of financial aid each year.

As a result, the differences between what some students could do and have outside the classroom and others could not became progressively more pronounced. Stanek was determined not just to acknowledge this reality but to confront it and force parents to think about it, too. "I felt it was necessary to take the bull by the horns and dive into this discussion," he said. "Everyone was saying that I was crazy, that no one should take this on in your second year as head of school." He did it anyway, leading a systematic, yearlong review of every instance throughout the school term when financial flexibility (or lack thereof) highlighted differences among students.

The middle school kids liked throwing bake sales. The intent was great, as it fostered building community and creating awareness of whatever cause they were raising money for. "But we'd also see that kids were comparing the money [they had] and buying for others, and would have big bills and use that as capital, showing off to friends and losing sight of what they had the money for," Stanek said. "There was one child who brought in a $100 bill." The school placed a $10 limit on what kids could spend.

The school's 5-times-per-year pizza lunch also began with the best of intentions. Usually all the kids bring their own lunch, so this, too, was a coming-together event that everyone looked forward to. But at $5 per lunch, it was $25 per year. That was a lot for some families, and other kids forgot to bring money. Then the faculty was left to sort out who had money and why or why not and who wasn't going to get to eat the pizza. "That raised issues around social class and access and exclusivity," Stanek said. Now, everyone eats and you just pay what you can. "There's no question about whether you are on the list," he added.

School logo gear is another domain where people with less money can feel uncomfortable. Every team understandably wants to do its own thing. "But how many times do parents need to be asked for another $25 or $40 to pay for the latest shirt in the latest season," Stanek wondered. The school decided to streamline and standardize, so that there was just one Shady Hill Athletics shirt each year, and every child got one for free since they're all required to play on at least one team. There is a website for parents who want to buy sweats and other gear. "But it's not in your face, where kids are put in a position where they and their parents have to make choices," Stanek said.

Sometime that year, he became aware of an eighth grader whose family had hired an expensive private counselor to help with high school applications. Others were hiring tutors to help with preparation for standardized tests that could help them get into the most competitive schools. Shady Hill didn't offer any test prep itself. "We don't believe in it," he said. "But not to acknowledge that it is going on is kind of naive. Did we need to get involved? What about the kids who can't afford test prep? Should we be doing more to help them?" The school ultimately decided not to help; staff there just couldn't get past their opposition to the tests altogether.

Now, Stanek hopes that the accumulation of changes and parental discussion about them has created a tilt toward more modesty that has become part of the school's brand. If it works, future applicant families will be self-selecting, doing a thorough values audit of all the schools they're considering before deciding to send kids to Shady Hill if they get in. "Parents have signed on because there isn't that emphasis on extravagance here," Stanek said.

His efforts are admirable, especially because they leave the school open to easy mockery. Isn't a $30,000 annual price tag itself an indulgence? And the head of school is worried about pizza and lettermen's jackets?! But to ignore the everyday reality of all his students would be to leave himself vulnerable to the adoption of the sort of casual vocabulary that has become standard at other schools. In affluent communities in California, both public and private school parents often refer to the February vacation as "ski week," even though plenty of families can't afford to gas up the car and head to Tahoe. The founder of one private school went so far as to change the dates of one of the winter breaks altogether so that the lines at his favorite ski lifts would be shorter. Teachers often pick up on this and do what they can to keep kids from feeling bad. In some schools, they no longer ask about anyone's vacation, because they realize that many kids' families can't afford to go on one.

Still, we don't want to pretend that differences don't exist. Social class is just another part of the diversity discussion, after all. Even Allison Pugh, the sociologist who wrote *Longing and Belonging* and coined the phrase "dignity gauntlet," understands that. "That moment of deprivation and indignity scares parents up and down the class ladder," she said. "They may remember their own experience of how often it happened to them and how much it hurt, and they want to protect their child from that moment. But they should relax. Kids manage that deprivation well. It's not bad for them to experience it. That's how I felt after three years of watching them."

The Materialism Intervention

Let's say you already have a couple of materialistic teenagers on your hands. It's not the end of the world. Tim Kasser, the materialism professor in Illinois, and a gang of other curious scholars decided to find out if it was possible to perform an intervention of sorts on older, upper-middle-class children—to actually manipulate materialism in a controlled experimental setting. And if they could, would any changes stick?

The group started by asking volunteer families in Minnesota to fill out questionnaires to determine who the truly materialistic children were. Then it randomly assigned the kids, ages 10 to 17, to two groups—one that would receive the intervention and one that would not. The idea was to measure their well-being over time to see if the reprogramming worked, and if so, for how long.

The intervention used a curriculum and a set of materials from a nonprofit organization called Share Save Spend. The kids met for three sessions, along with their parents. Session one included the distribution of a three-chamber bank (one each for sharing, saving, and spending) and discussion cards to inspire family conversations about money and values. There were also conversations about the difference between needs and wants, and the role advertising plays in confusing the two. The kids tracked their spending behavior and discussed it in session two. Then they kept a diary of the advertising messages they saw and their impact, and also interviewed people whom they thought modeled good sharing and saving. In session three, there was a discussion about allowance and how to keep the money conversation going among family members well into the future.

The researchers used surveys to measure the well-being of the participants six weeks after the last session. Then, they did it again 10 months later to see if any changes had actually stuck. Both times they found that the kids who had received the interventions showed better self-esteem than they had before the sessions started. The control group of materialistic kids who had not gone to the sessions showed decreased self-esteem. What is noteworthy here is not simply that the impact was lasting; it's that a program based on values and the emotions around money resonated with the older children especially. Detailed conversations and reflection seemed to make a real difference. Now, imagine all of us using this approach on an ongoing basis at home, and starting earlier.

Our own efforts could include stories about the times when we regretted a big purchase and others about objects with high prices that we cherish to this day. Our own tales, with real examples, can reduce some of the confusion our kids may feel about how our spending reflects our values.

The Dewey Rule: How Long to Make Kids Wait

Often, people who grow up in an environment that makes them feel insecure tend to default toward materialistic values. Twelve years after inheriting part of his father's secret real estate fortune, however, that's not how Bramson Dewey has turned out. His and his wife's cars do not raise any eyebrows in the upper-middle-class suburb where they live. He still has his $70 watch that he bought from Macy's many years ago and wears clothes that he buys at Kohl's.

He and his wife did treat the family to one expensive item: a house that's among the larger ones in the suburb where they live. They had been living in a smaller house but it got tight, so they moved to a larger one a few blocks away. Dewey admits to wondering what his girls, ages 6 and 10, will have to say as they begin to realize that their home is somewhat bigger than average homes in the area. His older daughter doesn't seem to notice so far. She came back from a trick-or-treating expedition agog at the fact that she got a full-size Hershey bar at one residence. "That's a rich person's house," she told her father.

Kids often operate under a completely different set of evaluative standards when it comes to relative wealth. Dewey's older daughter has a no-name fleece, while many kids at school wear North Face jackets. A classmate recently asked her if she was poor, given that her coat had no fancy logo.

Still, Dewey is certain that his older daughter knows that her parents will spring for things that are really worth owning or doing. "I, unlike my father, will happily open my wallet for reasonably priced necessities as well as some fun stuff," he said. "But I think it's important that they see that other kids have certain toys and games and that they themselves don't have everything. And that other families have fancy cars and take fancy trips to exotic islands."

When Dewey first put it this way to me, I got to wondering about something: Would it help some parents to have a rule based on whatever context they happen to find themselves in? I call it Dewey's rule, and it stands for the idea that parents should try to arrange things so that, on average, their children end up in the 30th percentile of stuff. If 10 kids in a community are eventually going to get a car, then your child should have the 7th nicest out of 10. Or if your children are in the 50th percentile on cars, then perhaps they should be 9th out of every 10 to get a smartphone. It's just a rough average to shoot for, not a hard-and-fast every-time law. And different parents may find themselves in special circumstances or may not have enough willpower to wait beyond, say, the 50th percentile. But kids should learn to wait for at least some things, to consider carefully the things they crave, and savor them once they arrive. Maybe it's fine to be a little jealous, while not feeling utterly deprived. Also, quite often, the thing that everyone thinks everyone else is going to want ends up being useless, or the kids who are the first-movers move on to something else by the time the 4th child out of 10 gets ready to mimic that first one. The child who is 5th or 7th, then, doesn't waste any money.

I've tested versions of the Dewey rule on many parents, and some of them blanch. Why not just have the courage of your convictions? they ask. Falling in line in such a regimented way is spineless. Perhaps there's some truth to that, and there are practical challenges to inventorying what other kids have and are doing once they're teenagers. Still, kids keep score in precisely this way. It's helpful to know where your family is on this continuum and whether your child has come to expect to be there consistently.

As for Dewey's feelings on the Dewey rule, he sees the wisdom of keeping something like it in mind. His house is always the 800-pound gorilla in the room. "I see myself as having to be a little more conscious about bringing everything else down so as to better average out to what you would call the 30th or 50th percent range," he said.

There is one final area where Bramson is dramatically different from his father. Mike wouldn't pay for most athletic activities, and he rarely came to any of Bramson's hockey games. But Bramson is different. He took his oldest daughter to the rink when she was 5. When she seemed to like it, he bought her skates without thinking too hard about the cost. Then the hockey gear. There were three helmets, because the first two weren't comfortable. And now he helps coach her team.

"For several nights a week during the season, it's me and my daughter and the other girls from her team on the ice," he said. "We pay for the whole season. We're together, having a great time. That's the spoiling. I like to think that she's thinking she's spoiled by how much time she gets with her family."

6

How to Talk About Giving

*Narrating your way through gifts of
$1, $1,000, and $1 million*

When Jewish teenagers turn 13, their congregations tra-
ditionally call them forward as a bar or bat mitzvah
to mark their entry into adulthood. They help lead a service in
temple on the Jewish Sabbath, they read in Hebrew from the
Torah, and they give a short speech about what they've learned
and what it all means to them. A photographer takes pictures,
grandparents cry, and the pubescent female guests tower over
boys whose voices have not yet begun to change.

But then the party starts, and the celebrations can get rather
elaborate. Sometimes, the kids themselves put on a show. Sam
Horowitz, a cherub-faced bar mitzvah boy from Dallas with
career aspirations in the entertainment industry, hit a make-
shift stage at the Omni Hotel there in 2012. With his name in
lights, each letter at least 15 feet high upstage, he descended
from the ceiling hidden inside what looked like a giant lamp-

shade. As the Jennifer Lopez song "Dance Again" blared from the sound system, he did just that, dressed entirely in white while surrounded by a bevy of professional female dancers in low-cut, gold-fringed dresses. A video of their well-rehearsed routine went viral, posted on YouTube by an entity called Elixir Entertainment, and many responses were stinging, including some from prominent rabbis. But Sam owned the moment and the many moments that followed, proudly appearing on Ellen Degeneres's television show not long after his big day to perform all over again. Ellen even gave him a gift—a sky-blue Jewish skullcap with her logo on it.

Parents like Michael Kesselman, who has worked in and around philanthropy for much of his career, have long wondered whether the coming-of-age tradition needed a radical reinvention. His children attended Brandeis Hillel Day School, a Jewish kindergarten-through-eighth-grade school in San Francisco. When I met him and some of the teachers in the school's conference room one sunny summer day, they were quick to note that the truly ostentatious parties hadn't happened in their community all that often. That sort of thing mostly happened in Los Angeles, they explained, sounding very Northern Californian.

Kesselman was moved to act not after an outsize celebration but after he asked his eldest daughter, several years out from her bat mitzvah, whether she remembered any of the gifts her friends had purchased for her. She managed to recall just one or two. When another daughter's 13th birthday approached, he rounded up some like-minded parents for a little "thinking and figuring," as they put it in a letter to their fellow seventh-grade moms and dads. There were 33 seventh graders. Each family spent at least $20 for a gift for each of those students on their big day, given that every student would invite all the others to their individual celebrations. Collectively, parents were spending $21,780 on gifts throughout the year, at a minimum.

In their letter to fellow parents, they proposed an alternative. They could pool all that money and divide it up, with each child getting a small sum and a gift, and the rest going into a single pile of money for the kids to give away to any charity they chose. The grown-ups would have nothing to do with the selection. Instead, it would be the teenagers who would run a foundation and listen to pitches from nonprofit executives who wanted a grant from their fund.

Explaining Why and How We Give

It's not surprising that someone like Kesselman, who had worked for foundations himself, dreamed up something like this. Parents have an essential role to play in modeling generosity, and researchers have shown that if parents give, kids tend to as well. Most important, it helps if parents talk to their offspring about giving too. And the more parents give, the greater the likelihood that they talk to their kids about that giving. (The same thing is true for volunteering, by the way.)

If you haven't primed this pump of generosity with your kids by talking to them about your own charitable giving, you're not alone. In 2010 the financial education arm of a large insurance company ran a poll and asked kids 17 and under how their parents support organizations and causes. Some of them knew a little bit, with 18 percent saying their parents volunteer, 10 percent saying they donate money, and 6 percent reporting that their folks gave food, clothing, and supplies. But 64 percent of the kids said they had no idea what their parents were giving, if anything. "Clueless," the company called the kids in its headline on the press release.

So why the silence? It may be that parents fail to initiate any memorable conversations about why giving is a good idea in the first place. Our giving may become rote, and once it does, we may not bother explaining our own generosity to our kids.

But because we're in the business of cultivating grown-ups here, giving, like everything else that we do with money, shouldn't simply happen without comment. Correcting this is easy enough, and there are at least three ways to explain why giving money to help other people is a good thing to do. One way to describe it is as a sort of duty; families who have more than they need ought to give something so that families who have very little can have more of the things that they need but can't afford. This has the added benefit of reinforcing the Wants/Needs framework with younger children by bringing it into another area of a family's financial life.

Older children might also appreciate a second explanation, which is a self-interested one; research on happiness shows that the amount we give away is a great predictor of how happy we are. In fact, it's as strong a predictor of happiness as our income is. Finally, there's this point to make: Communities are stronger when people know they can rely on one another. We would all feel better knowing that we live in a neighborhood, city, country, and world where we will help others when they're having a hard time and they will help us if we need it. Perhaps we live in such places already and have given and gotten in a way that has proven it. Still, giving generously when we can helps reinforce our common bonds.

Like many conversations with kids about money, we don't need to have this one all that often. But we could probably start talking about giving earlier, as children are hardwired for the happiness-making part of generosity from a very early age. One delightful study that makes this point is "Giving Leads to Happiness in Young Children," where the authors of the study ran their experiment on 20-month-old toddlers. The team of experimenters recruited parents from libraries, hospitals, and community events in Vancouver, Canada. When the toddlers were the right age, their parents brought them to a lab where they got to play with puppets. Why puppets? Because they delight kids. Unfamiliar humans can make them feel inhibited or cause them to act in a particular way because they think the grown-ups expect a certain kind of behavior.

The puppets and the kids each got a bowl with a Teddy Graham or a Goldfish cracker in it. The kids were told they could eat their treat if they wanted and that the puppets liked treats too. To reinforce this point, the puppets pretended that they were eating by pushing their treats through a false bottom in their bowls while making happy "yum" sounds.

Then, a new puppet arrived on the scene named Monkey. The experimenter pointed out that neither Monkey nor the child subject had any treats. The experimenter presented 8 new treats and deposited them in the child's bowl. Next, the experimenter found another treat and gave it to Monkey. After that, yet another treat appeared, but this time the experimenter asked the toddler to give that *new* treat to Monkey. Finally, the experimenter asked the toddler to hand over treats from his or her *own* bowl, where the original 8 treats still sat. This experiment was repeated over and over with different children. All along, observers were keeping a close eye on the toddlers' faces to score their precise reactions.

So what did they discover? The toddlers were happier when giving a treat to the puppets than they were when the experimenters dumped a pile of them into their own bowls. But that wasn't all; the kids were actually happier giving away their own treats from the original stash of 8 than they were giving away the new one that they had gotten later. In other words, they were actually more excited about giving away things that were *costly*—the treats that were their own, in theory—than they were about giving away the windfall treat that only "belonged" to them for a brief moment in time.

But do toddlers simply learn this behavior along the way and mimic it? When I called up one of the study's coauthors, Kiley Hamlin, a psychology professor at the University of British Columbia, she pointed out a couple of things. Yes, toddlers see plenty of people being nice to them, but if they have older siblings, they may see plenty of the opposite behavior as well. "What tells me that the generosity isn't basic mimicry is how early they start giving stuff to people," she said. "Most 12-month-olds will sit with you and insist that you take their gross Cheerios, over and over. And insist that you eat them, and like them. It's not just that they want to give them to you; they want to watch and make sure you enjoy it." She believes simple evolution is the explanation here: We live in groups for protection and companionship, and doing so requires cooperation and generosity.

The Homeless Question and How to Handle It

As with many of the most important money conversations, it can be hard to find the right moment to introduce the giving topic. Kids, however, will make up their own minds on timing, and it's often when something right before their eyes is confusing or troubling.

One autumn afternoon in 1991, a playwright named Teddy Gross was walking in Manhattan when his 4-year-old daughter Nora spotted a homeless man. He had newspapers wadded in his shoes to protect his feet from the elements, and he was sitting on a busy sidewalk leaning up against a newsstand. Gross wasn't in the habit of giving money to panhandlers and didn't even see the man at first. But his daughter spotted him and sized him up, and the man smiled at her. And while the family had never had a conversation about homeless people before, Nora knew just what the man's problem was and how best to solve it. So she turned to her father and asked him a question.

"Can we take him home?"

Most of us who live near homeless people or regularly pass through or visit places where they ask for money have been in this spot, even if our own children's questions were a little different. A child might ask why we give money to strangers who ask for it. Or, alternatively, they demand to know why we don't. They may also want to know why homeless people have no place to live or whether it's their fault or their choice. For parents, these moments tend to be ones of hyperconsciousness and wildly mixed feelings. There is pride in the fact that a child recognizes the humanity of others and is moved to act. Shame if we don't give ourselves or if we turn away. Anger or fear if a panhandler is aggressive or scares our children. Frustration with a society where people live on the streets. And, perhaps most of all, there's confusion about the best way to explain the complicated answers and all our feelings about them to kids of varying ages.

It would have been easy enough for Teddy to brush off his daughter's question or treat it as a rhetorical one. He could have lied and said no, even though it was certainly possible to take the man back to their apartment for a meal or a shower or a few nights on their sofa. He could have told the truth and said yes— but then explained that it was risky because homeless people are sometimes mentally ill and can behave unpredictably. He could have ducked the question, telling her that her idea was a really nice one and that they could talk about it later.

But none of those answers would have been very satisfying. "Children's early years are characterized by a compulsion to find out, a strong urge to both map out and transform reality," according to Susan Engel, a senior lecturer in psychology at Williams College and an expert on curiosity. So what was Nora trying to map out? Well, embedded in her question was probably a fair bit of confusion about a lot of things. Why didn't the man have a home? What did people on the sidewalks do with the money they asked for? Why didn't her parents simply take in every stranger in need? How much could her family reasonably do and be expected to do to alleviate the suffering of others? As for her desire to transform reality, to her the solution was obvious: They could take in that man and make his life better.

Nora's question cut to her father's core. He remembers being shocked that she recognized the sadness of the situation and frustrated with his inability to respond well in the moment. "These questions are momentous occasions," he said. "But I couldn't answer in any way that was satisfying. There was a feeling that if I didn't listen to her, the day might come when I would regret it, where she'd want to know where I was when all those homeless people were crowding the streets." So his response was to collect money to help the homeless return to homes of their own. First, they walked around their apartment building to collect people's loose change. Then they solicited further, eventually starting an organization called the Common Cents Penny Harvest that has collected $10 million from schoolchildren and others in the years since.

This is not to say that we all need to run out and start organizations every time our children ask a stunning question. But it's a reminder that they are capable of deep, penetrating inquiries about how money touches so much of life. Teddy Gross was right about the lack of a perfect answer here, though some responses are unwise. A younger child's question about homeless people shouldn't cause you to criticize the people who are asking for help, assuming they're not threatening you or your child. Whatever you may think of people who live on the streets and ask others for help, a child who isn't in grade school yet isn't ready to wrestle with the roots of homelessness and urban housing policy.

As always, do your best not to lie, either. Why did you give that man money? Because he needed help. Why does he need help? He doesn't seem to have a place to live right now or enough money for food. Why not? It's hard to know, but we try to help people who are having a hard time, both when we see them and by sending money to other people and groups who can help them even more.

I didn't used to give money to people who asked for it on the street, but a commenter on a blog post I wrote for *The New York Times'* website caused me to reconsider. "I really don't care what they spend it on, and I don't care if they're conning me or whatever," the commenter said. "I really do care about teaching my son compassion and empathy for others. That's worth the spare change." Now, if I'm with my daughter and someone asks us for help, I look the person in the eye, say "good luck," and hand over a bit of money. "To ignore the homeless guy is to teach [kids] to ignore other people who are hurting," as Eileen and Jon Gallo put it in their book *Silver Spoon Kids.*

An Easy Family Project:
The Giving Bag

One reason many of us dislike giving money directly to homeless people is that we can't be sure how they will spend it. Olivia Higgins, who lives in Oakland, California, and is the mother of two, knows this especially well. Before she moved there to work as a teacher and administrator, she worked at a women's shelter in Philadelphia. Given her experience as an educator and case manager, it's hard to imagine someone better suited to talk to children about helping the homeless. But even she was flummoxed by her two children, ages 7 and 9, and their constant requests to give money to the homeless people they frequently encountered.

After hearing about a friend who asked her first-grade students to assemble small bags for a local food bank, she hit on an idea. First, the family held a yard sale. To convince the children to contribute old toys, she told them they could keep half the proceeds and that the family would give the rest away. This was an important point for Higgins, since she wanted her children to use money they'd earned themselves so that they could get a more visceral sense of what it meant to give. At first, the kids wanted to simply hand out the money to homeless people, but Higgins told them more about her old job and why cash might not be helpful. They were able to grasp the basic idea of addiction and listened to her stories about how addicts at the shelter who had money were often tempted to buy drugs and alcohol.

The family settled on the idea of using the money to give away bags of supplies to anyone they encountered who might need one. When it came time to assemble them from the proceeds of the garage sale, the two kids had strong feelings about the contents. The conversations that ensued made Higgins realize just how deeply they had been thinking about the homeless. "My daughter was determined to include one permanent marker, so they could write their signs," she said. "My son wanted to include a little notebook because he thought they always looked bored. He really wanted to include playing cards, but they ultimately decided against that because it would be too sad if they were alone and didn't have anyone to play with." The bags also had some food inside, including a bit of leftover Halloween candy.

One unexpected result of Higgins's addiction explanation was her daughter's desire to include notes in the bags urging people to stay off drugs. "Katherine challenged me on this point quite a bit," Higgins said. "Her argument was that a good message is a good message, and who cares where it comes from? I'm not sure I did an adequate job of explaining why a grown person experiencing a difficult situation probably doesn't want to hear an antidrug message from a kid in a minivan with leather seats."

So the family distributed the bags with markers but no anti-drug notes. One of the first went to a man who saw the paper bag when the family approached him and thought he was about to receive a peanut butter sandwich. He explained that he didn't like peanut butter, but he told the children that it reminded him of his mother, whom he hadn't seen for some time. They had a nice conversation, and as they drove away, Higgins's son, Dylan, said that he thought it had been a lovely way to make a new friend.

For those of us who don't have a car to lug bags around in or commute by public transportation with our children, there are other things we can keep in our bags to give out. Protein bars or other compact, hardy, and nutrient-dense edibles are items that a child could hand to a person who is asking for help. Gift cards to discount stores or fast-food restaurants would work as well. The point is to have something we can always reach for that will make it easy to say yes to someone in need and will make most recipients feel good about the help we're offering. Some people may turn down food or gift cards, so be ready to explain to a child why that might be and whether they want to give money instead, either to those individuals or to organizations that can help them.

Small Children, Solicitations, and the Importance of Showing Up in Person

There are many other ways to encourage regular conversations around giving. Storing allowance money in a Give jar along with the Spend and Save ones will help. Its presence reminds younger children to think about causes they might want to support, particularly if you empty it out on a regular basis, say every six months, and ask your kids to pick an organization to support right then.

Two tactics can help make the giving experience more meaningful. First, try to give money in the kids' names once in a while, even if it means losing out on a tax deduction. Once this happens, they'll start getting their own solicitation mail. Not only do many children love getting letters when they're first learning to read, but it's fascinating to see how young children respond to the pitches and the perks.

Bruce Kimmel, a father of three in Saint Paul, Minnesota, started having his kids give at an early age. Not only did they love getting the mail, they were also hooked by the conservation organization that sent out stuffed toy lemurs to children who gave $50 or more. In contrast, the local zoo sent only mail and no gifts, so it dropped off the kids' giving list. It's completely normal for kids to be swayed and probably harmless in the moment. But offering the gifts isn't all that dissimilar to the tactics that I see credit card companies and brokerage firms using in my work as a personal finance columnist, where they offer tens of thousands of frequent flier miles to potential customers. Point out to children when they're being manipulated this way, just so they begin to recognize these offers and rewards as the marketing pitches that they are.

The second tactic to use with younger children is for them to give the money in person. This will work only with local organizations, but it's worth doing at least once; one study has shown that smaller kids are much more likely to be generous when they know that somebody else is watching. If the choice is a zoo or a museum or a school or a shelter, call up the development office and ask if they'd mind accepting a donation from a child in person. My daughter decided to give six months of her accumulated Give money to a nonprofit that raises money for research on hearing loss. Her cousin is hearing-impaired, and I'm not sure I'll ever forget the look on my sister-in-law's face when my daughter handed over the money. Hopefully, my daughter won't either.

Next Step: Giving Without Benefits

After a few years of giving, consider introducing a new challenge that I learned about from Catherine Newman, who blogs about her two children from Amherst, Massachusetts. Like the Kimmel kids who loved the lemurs they got in exchange for their donations, Newman's daughter enjoyed the stuffed otter that she got for giving to the World Wildlife Federation. Eventually, the family instituted a rule that required at least some of their kids' giving budget go to helping people. Animals are cute and easy to care about; thinking about humans in need is hard. But part of the point of the exercise here is to ask kids to consider the hardships of others. Whether these gifts are local ones to food banks or homeless shelters or donations to global organizations, they benefit people who probably have much less than our kids do. Whenever children can grasp that idea, we should ask them to increase the portion of their Give money that goes to organizations that help other people we do not know directly.

This is often a harder thing for adults to accomplish than it is for kids. About one-third of all charitable donations in the United States go to the religious institutions where we worship. That money supports plenty of good deeds, whether it's making services available to all comers or doing work in the larger community and the world. Still, it's at least partly self-interested; the tax-deductible contributions give us a place to bow our heads and reflect with paid clergy who may also provide religious instruction to our children. Plenty more money goes to our various alma maters. Some of it replenishes the scholarship funds that allowed us to afford these schools in the first place, so it feels like a moral obligation to give. But that money is not helping the people in the world who need it most, at least not directly.

There is no hypocrisy in setting one giving rule for children as a teaching exercise and having different guidelines for ourselves. Part of what we're trying to do as our kids approach adolescence is help them consider the lives of people outside their own small community. Once they do, however, they'll begin to question our own charitable choices, especially if we're giving plenty of money to organizations that we have a stake in. So be forewarned. Still, this questioning of priorities is something we should welcome, and there's one great way to invite the conversation as they grow older.

Letting Children Participate
in the Charity Budget

The best way to help kids learn about giving is to give them a literal seat at the table when the grown-ups make decisions about donations. This may involve some adjustments in our routine. It also means making an actual household giving budget and thinking about it as one large pie that we divide consciously and conscientiously.

Start by reviewing last year's numbers, as my wife and I recently did with our daughter, who had just turned 8. We didn't tell her the dollar amounts, and she didn't ask, though we probably will give her the totals in a few years. Instead, we took 100 dried beans and put them on the dining room table. Then we took some scratch paper and made labels representing all the organizations we had supported the previous year. A donation to provide malaria nets in developing countries accounted for about 25 percent of our giving, so we moved 25 beans next to that label. We repeated this with all of the beans and all of the donations. As we did so, we explained to her how we had heard of the organization (if she wasn't already aware of it) and why it was important to us.

Next, we handed over a pile of mail, all the solicitations that had arrived from charitable organizations in the previous three months. One surprise was how our daughter applied her understanding of wants and needs to the giving conversation. A solicitation from a public art fund didn't pass muster with her because she didn't think that new statues in a park were a true need. She also rejected a solicitation from an organization where she'd once taken dance lessons, because it didn't explain how it would help kids who could not afford the fees. Using similar logic, she wanted to support a scholarship fund at her camp to help other kids attend. She did not question too many of my wife's and my priorities, so we did not need to rearrange many of the beans to make her feel included. We know that challenges from her will come in time though.

Watching my daughter's mind work in this way was one of the highlights of the holiday season for me, even if I didn't always agree with her choices. We ended up turning over less than 5 percent of the giving budget to her and plan to increase it bit by bit in future years. For families with one child, there isn't much negotiation involved. Families with two or more kids will need a system for decision making, though it could also be fun to let the kids sort it out themselves. Can they come to a consensus and perhaps have more impact with a larger donation to fewer organizations? Or will they split the kids' portion of the budget among themselves and make their own decisions? Ask them to explain themselves and report back on the organizations they chose and why. What swayed them about a local organization as opposed to a global one? Why disease, say, and not poverty?

Laura Sundquist, a financial planner who lives in New Hartford, Connecticut, has taken a different approach, making giving a more regular event. On January 1, each of her two sons gets 12 checks for a modest amount of money with the line for "Pay to the Order of" left blank. Each month, they think about a cause that's important to them and send the check off. She tries to encourage them to learn a bit about the organization they're sending money to as well. One of her sons is a cancer survivor and has given money to a research organization in that area.

The boys have also donated to a town fund that helps people in need, U.S. soldiers in Afghanistan, a group that raises awareness of Down syndrome (which a cousin was born with) and a jog-a-thon to raise money to build a new playground. With regular practice, they seem to have settled on an eclectic mix of charitable organizations that touch them personally and do good deeds for people they do not know.

Consider taking the blank-check approach to gift giving when a holiday or birthday rolls around. One approach my family has tried is to gift three checks to the kids in our extended circle, along with a short explanation. One check that we write is for the recipient's college savings fund, if we're reasonably sure that it isn't going to be easy for the family to pay for college themselves. Another goes toward a bit of mad money that the recipient can spend on anything at all. The third check has the "To" part left blank, with instructions to send it to an organization that needs it and a request to let us know which cause got the money and why.

How Much to Give, and of What

Once giving becomes a regular activity in families, the topic will probably come up spontaneously on a fairly regular basis. For those of us who want to stoke the conversation a bit, we can make a ritual of talking about something we did that day or that week that helped someone else. Who was it? Why did we do it? How did it make us feel? For parents who are weary of the monosyllabic answers our kids give when we're actually able to sit down for dinner as a family, the conversation starters from the Central Carolina Community Foundation may be helpful. Its "Talk About Giving" box comes with dozens of cards with a single provocative question on each:

"What is our family's history of helping?"
"What do you appreciate most about our town?"
"If we were to live on less money, what could we do without?"
"What's something you're willing to do without right now?"

Those last two questions can be particularly consequential, since your kids may surprise you with what they're willing to give up. If you decide to honor their request, it could change all of your lives. This is what happened to Kevin Salwen, a journalist, and his wife, Joan King Salwen, a consultant-turned-educator, when their Atlanta-based family first started having serious discussions about giving. They didn't have many dinnertime rituals during their first 14 years as parents besides asking someone to say a quick blessing. It was accomplishment enough that the family managed to dine together at all most nights, even if the conversation often centered on the logistical puzzle of getting their teenage daughter, Hannah, and her younger brother, Joseph, to their various activities. They came home each day to a 6,500-square-foot house complete with Corinthian columns and an elevator that led to Hannah's bedroom. People walking through the neighborhood often stopped to take pictures.

The family was charitable, giving away about 3 percent of its income each year, but the parents wrote the checks and the kids didn't know much about it. Still, there was no reason for Joan and Kevin to think that the kids were brooding over whether they were fully meeting their responsibilities to their fellow human beings. But one day, as Hannah and her father pulled up to a stoplight next to a large Mercedes and spotted a homeless man on the street, she made an observation. "If that man had a less nice car, that man there could have a meal," she said. Kevin sensed that he hadn't heard the last from her on the topic, and sure enough, she brought it up that night at dinner. "She wanted to know why we were not better participants in closing the world's disparities," Kevin said, sitting across from Joan in an interview 6 years after that meal. "We all slowed down to think about where we were."

Joan and Kevin soon realized that their giving hadn't made any impact on their kids. At first, they were defensive with their daughter and tried to list all the checks they had written, but they realized how that sounded. "Soulless" is how Kevin described it. "We needed something the kids could feel." Hannah kept questioning their commitment and generosity, and eventually, Joan pushed back.

"What do you want to do?" she asked her daughter. "Sell our house? Move into a smaller one and give what's left over to charity?"

Yes, in fact. That's exactly what Hannah wanted to do.

With the benefit of hindsight, Hannah's parents can see hints of what led to her strong feelings in general, and about money and justice in particular. Some of it was nature; she had been literally an outward-facing baby, preferring to look out at the world from her Baby Björn. Her parents read her and her brother stories aloud from the newspaper that raised complicated ethical questions. They encouraged her to work, and she babysat and had a business making blankets. She volunteered at a food bank, and her parents let her work at a restaurant for homeless people, though they did check it out for safety first. She also loved *Chicken Soup for the Soul* stories.

"She would memorize them," Joan recalled.

"The more saccharine, the better," Kevin added, as they both broke out laughing.

So perhaps Joan should have known better than to push Hannah's buttons with what amounted to a dare. "Maybe another parent would have said 'OK, that's enough, we've explained our generosity and our involvement in the community, and it's time to drop it,'" she said. "In a way, this was my way of saying that: 'For heaven's sake, how far do you want to go?'" Except Hannah really did want to go halfway to zero, cutting her family's living space to a still generous 3,000 square feet or so and giving away whatever was left over after they sold one house and bought another.

Now, put yourself in Joan and Kevin's shoes as a parent. At the time, they had no mortgage and knew they had enough saved for retirement and college that giving away half of the equity in their home wouldn't destroy them financially as long as neither one of them got sick or injured. And they'd managed to raise a child committed enough to the world to give up a bit of comfort for whatever good might come from that sacrifice. Shouldn't they be proud? How much could they learn together if they said yes? And how much fun would it be to give a bunch of money away now, instead of in a will when they were dead, or to some future grandchildren that they might not live to see?

So they said yes. They put the house on the market for just under $2 million, bought another for $962,000, and ended up giving nearly $1 million through a six-year pledge, even though the original house sold for only $1.4 million amid a real estate downturn. They would not tell me (and still haven't told their kids) what percentage of their net worth that contribution represented, but they did not have to put Hannah's or Joseph's college tuition at risk.

As for what they did with the money, figuring it out was a large enough project that Kevin and Hannah wrote a book about it called *The Power of Half,* easily the most inspiring work I read during the years I spent researching this book. Right away, they established that all four of them were going to have full and equal voting rights on where and how they would give the money away. They agreed that any project should meet the following specifications: They wanted to solve one problem completely, see a project through to completion, have the project be in Africa, work with an organization that had expertise in the area and that allowed the recipients to control the donation. Ultimately, they decided to pay for two epicenters in Ghana and the staff that would work there—buildings that serve as meeting halls, micro-lending banks, food-storage facilities, and health centers that include small residences for nurses. With the help of experts, they saw the projects through, including training for the staff, and visited the completed buildings.

"Only now do we look back at our old life and marvel at what we used to be," Kevin said, six years out from Joan's challenge and Hannah's (and, eventually, Joseph's) affirmative response. "I don't think we were bad parents or a bad family, but we were so far from whole. What we gained outstripped what we had, in terms of the closeness of our family relationships, in terms of the richness of our lives. We got to go to Africa, to understand how subsistence farmers live and the kinds of decisions they make, how extraordinarily creative they are, when all we would have done otherwise is read about it in a book. Our lives are so much fuller now. I don't think it's even close." Joan is still an educator, while Kevin writes and is a board member for organizations like Habitat for Humanity and Year Up.

When you give away half your home equity and write a book about the experience, it's natural to hope that other people will be inspired to do their own good works. And once *The Power of Half* was published in 2010, a handful of other similar initiatives did spring into action. After hearing about the Salwens, a lawyer in Los Angeles named Tony Tolbert moved in with his mother and handed over his house keys to a local homeless family. They stayed in his home for a year. "It's the damn most flattering thing I've ever heard," Kevin Salwen said.

Tolbert is single, but there is at least one family that also traded down after hearing about the book. The Solimene family lived in Barrington, Illinois, a suburb where equestrian-minded Chicago families often keep their horses. Husband Mick grew up middle class, earned an MBA at the University of Chicago, and forged a successful career in finance, working with troubled companies. Wife Keely came from a family that struggled financially, though she never realized that she lacked anything. "When I went to college, I began to understand that shoes came in boxes and didn't come looped with a piece of plastic at Zayre," the local discount store, she said.

The pair had four children in fairly rapid succession, and the first big twist of generosity in their lives came when they heard about a 3-year-old girl in a Vietnamese orphanage. At the time, their youngest child was already in grade school, and some friends who had recently adopted themselves heard that this girl was available for adoption as well. She was an excellent soccer player; Mick was an ex-player himself.

"We had no plans, adoption or otherwise," for additional children, Keely recalled. But they decided to try to adopt the girl anyway. Once it was clear that they would be approved to take the child home, it also became apparent that separating the soccer player from a younger girl in the orphanage who she had bonded with was going to be intensely traumatic. So the Solimenes adopted them both in 2002.

In the years since, they have returned to Vietnam often; on one trip they discovered that one of their new daughters had a twin sister elsewhere in the country. In 2008, they tracked her down and the two now Skype every weekend. The Solimenes have given money to the orphanage and to support their daughter's twin and her family.

But when Keely read *The Power of Half,* something clicked for both her and Mick. "We were spending lots of time in a country where the citizens and twin sister of our daughter were living in circumstances nothing like what we're living in," Mick said. He was tiring of his long commute to downtown Chicago and the long drives back and forth to the nearest airport for business trips. Keely ached to do even more good for the world. And so they chose to move from the land of horse stables to Arlington Heights, a suburb with smaller lots and sidewalks. Mick's Porsche went back to the dealer around the same time, a car that both parents now refer to as "that car that began with *P.*"

The family gives generously to the United Nations Foundation. And while the kids were not involved with the initial decision to downsize, most of the siblings are intimately involved with a venture that the family has funded with the money that the move helped free up. It's called Bella Ha, named for Isabella, the twin in Arlington Heights, and her sister, Ha, in Vietnam. Starting in 2015, the business will sell sandals and use the proceeds to pay for solar power installations at maternity clinics around the world that are off the electrical grid.

The move confused many neighbors and old friends, and some of them seemed to take offense. Keely said they shouldn't have. "What we did was really quite personal," she said. "We didn't want to offend anyone. I don't believe that money or affluence is the enemy at all. Everyone is on his or her own personal journey, and I don't want to be that family that ditched all those people who were a negative influence on their kids. Ultimately, we believe that we are the influence on our kids."

When the family moved, it took two trucks to transport their belongings. Only one made it to Arlington Heights. The second was for things they gave away. And this is the framed maxim that the Solimenes chose to hang on the kitchen wall: "If you want to feel rich, just count all the gifts you have that money can't buy."

The School Where Giving Replaces Getting

At the Brandeis Hillel Day School, in San Francisco, the proposal to make the bar and bat mitzvah process more about giving drew a lot of positive response. As one parent put it, pooling the money in a fund for the kids to give away relieved them of spending a bunch of time and money on buying gifts that didn't really make a difference, even to the recipients. The lessons in generosity sounded pretty nice too, which is what Michael Kesselman—the philanthropy expert who, with his wife, first thought of the fund—and the other parents emphasized in a note they sent to their fellow seventh-grade parents. "We believe that we should take advantage of our being a community to underline and emphasize the less materialistic aspects of this very significant marker in the life of a Jewish person," they wrote.

A few parents, though, took the mention of materialism personally. "We had one parent—of a large, wealthy family—whose first son was becoming a bar mitzvah, and they were looking forward to its being a really big deal," Kesselman recalled. "The father was in tears. He said our underlying message is that if you're going to do a big blowout, then you're going to be embarrassed." This is not at all surprising. Anyone trying to change or create a standard in a community that has something to do with how families spend money will probably run into some resistance, even if the shift is as virtuous as this one seemed to be.

Still, nearly all of the families ultimately agreed to participate. Those without a lot of spare money simply paid what they could. A few families opted for a more traditional gift-giving approach, though families were welcome to give an individual gift to a special friend on top of contributing to the fund. "It wasn't like the Soviet Union or something, where we said that you couldn't give a gift," Kesselman said.

All the students participated in managing the fund, even if their families had chosen not to contribute. They created a letterhead with all of their names on it, and they all signed every bit of correspondence with an organization that was asking them for money. The letters from the fund's early days look like the sign-in poster boards that many families put up on easels at the entrance to their parties, with 33 bits of loopy seventh-grade cursive on each note. The fund had typed agendas for its meetings and treasurer reports too, just like a normal foundation.

From the start, the students agreed on a majority-rules vote for each funding request. And while Michael Kesselman, himself an experienced foundation staffer, hung around to help, he tried not to intervene. "I sat down with the kids and told them that I worked for them and that they were going to make the decisions about whom to fund," he said.

The seventh graders met at lunch, and one of their first visitors was Justin Grosso, who worked as bagger in a grocery store and was enrolled in trade school. He was looking for an additional sponsor for his participation in the California AIDS bicycle ride. At that point, Kesselman reached into his bag of fund-raising tricks and explained the idea of a challenge grant to the kids. Not long after, they promised Grosso $500 if he could raise an additional $1,000 on his own. He met the goal and then some.

Almost immediately, according to Kesselman, the students were asking questions as good as those of any adult. The mere act of evaluating proposals from older people, with something of consequence at stake, is something that kids do not get to do much in any context. The students took to it quickly.

They also loved the big reveal, according to Batshir Torchio, who spent years teaching at the school and recently became a rabbi. "When my class allotted $3,000 to the local Boys and Girls club, the woman who took our call wanted to know if it was a joke," she said. "She got the director of the program on the phone to speak to our students. The director burst into tears."

The school eventually made the fund permanent, incorporating it into the seventh-grade curriculum, with the goal of helping students understand the systemic causes of poverty, what it means to be poor, who the poor are, and how to improve the world by addressing the root causes of poverty (and not merely by giving money to organizations that help people who need it). In addition to making budgets and grilling executives from local nonprofits, the children also dove into an eclectic collection of texts four times each week. Their readings included selections from Barbara Ehrenreich's *Nickel and Dimed*, various parts of the Bible and the Talmud, and the full text of municipal ballot measures on the minimum wage and panhandling.

The teachers also started dividing the class into pretend families. Each would have a different income and series of events they had to deal with. If an adult in the household lost a job, they had to figure out how the grocery budget would change. Students created a shopping list for a family of four living at the poverty level and trying to purchase a month's worth of groceries. They walked to the nearest grocery store to make the purchases (and eventually to donate the food to the local food bank). Most of them had no idea how much food a family needs each month, but they soon learned.

Today, nearly 20 years after Michael Kesselman first suggested the idea to his fellow parents, the Seventh-Grade Fund remains at the core of the middle school experience at Brandeis Hillel. "It's part of the culture of the school now," said Neal Biskar, a veteran teacher and administrator there. It's part of the culture elsewhere, too, as schools, synagogues, and other Jewish organizations across the country have copied it in various ways.

And there's no reason any school, religious or not, couldn't adapt it for its own use as well.

The beauty of the fund is that it does not require outsize sacrifice from most families. They made a decision, as a community, that their kids had plenty of gifts and could give some of what they had to others. Kevin and Joan King Salwen had more than enough house, and their daughter, Hannah, inspired them to give some of it away in effect. But Kevin takes pains to make sure that nobody walks away from a conversation with him thinking that he wants every family to make the same gift or one of similar financial size. "We've never been about people selling their houses," he said. "We know that's goofy."

Maybe your kids have too much time on their hands, or too many clothes, or something else. Perhaps you could take half of your dining-out budget and use it to make a family gift to an organization that helps people who don't have enough to eat. Or you could do something similar with your vacation budget. And maybe, if you pull the right strings or press the right buttons, your own school can help turn a similar idea into a movement.

"This has been one of the most meaningful things I've ever participated in as a teacher," Batshir Torchio said of her time helping the seventh graders with their giving. "I'm doing the Snoopy dance all day long."

7

Why Kids Should Work

Lessons from farm work, mandatory tuition payments, and a unified theory of tin can redemption

As I traveled the country meeting parents and kids and talking about money the last few years, I was surprised at the number of parents who told me stories, unprompted, about boys and girls redeeming cans and bottles. Children get the idea from watching strangers on the street collecting recyclables and ask their parents how it works, or they watch family members redeem cans at the grocery store. Others read the refund notices on drink containers and want in on the 5-cent-per-unit action, and beg their parents for a ride to the recycling center or ask to drag a wagon on their own.

What is it about the recycling-for-money routine that so appeals to children? To find out, I spent an afternoon with the Clarke family in San Jose, California. They live on the side of a hill with a backyard where Julie, who does marketing for a technology company, and her husband, Gary, a teacher and football coach, regularly entertain. Their two daughters, Katherine, age 11, and Lauren, 7, earn spending money from the work they do around the house, like many other kids their age.

But not long ago, they picked up a side gig. The idea was born from their church's campaign to raise money for the homeless, which encouraged parishioners to bring cans and bottles to church for recycling. The church campaign eventually ended, but by then the two Clarke daughters were hooked on collecting and sorting, and the cash reward it provided. Could they keep doing it, they asked, and keep the money for themselves? Their parents wanted them to continue giving some recycling proceeds to the church, but they were also keenly aware of the number of things the girls wanted to buy. So they found a scrapyard a freeway ride away that would accept the contents of their bins. Now, every time the girls have collected enough to fill the back of their minivan, they set off with a parent to redeem what they have collected.

After a 20-minute drive from their home, the Clarke family minivan pulls into the driveway of Ranch Town Recycling Center, in San Jose, and Katherine and Lauren jump from their seats and lift out bags of glass bottles, aluminum cans, and assorted plastic. It's September, warm enough that the center is especially ripe with the odor of everything that used to be inside the recycled materials. People walk every which way as forklifts beep, employees toss the bags of cans and bottles around, and a man with a cigarette dangling from his mouth runs a machine that crunches glass, shooting a few shards within striking distance of customers who get too close. The patriarch of the family who runs the center weighs the bags on a scale, the matriarch runs the cash register, and the employees yell at anyone and everyone who doesn't quite know the drill. On the way home the family usually stops at Merriwest Credit Union so the girls can deposit the money they receive for their recyclables.

The response from other grown-ups when kids go to redeem cans and bottles tends to be mixed. The Clarkes contend with logistics, including keeping the cans and bottles clean so they won't attract vermin, making space to store them all, and then taking the lot away to exchange it for money. Julie Clarke's friend Aleksandra Gradinarova has a can collector in her house too, though her feelings about it are mixed, due to personal history.

Gradinarova and her husband grew up in Communist Bulgaria, but left there as young adults and now work in the technology industry. There wasn't much to buy when they were children, but their 4-year-old son, Nikola, is growing up in an American world filled with toys. Like many boys his age, he asks to buy more, frequently. "Every day," Aleksandra said. His father finally explained to him that if they bought all the toys he wanted, there wouldn't be any money left for him to go to college. This was a problem, since he was already aware that big kids in college get to have laptop computers. He wanted to be one of them, so he quickly changed tactics and sought money he could save to go to college. Presented with this opening, his father told him stories from the old country about turning beer bottles in for money. Nikola loved this idea. Soon the pair were hauling bags to the grocery store and exchanging them for piles of quarters.

This wasn't the most comfortable thing for Aleksandra, however, who told me that she was worried that people would wonder about her. "What is the first thing that pops into your head when you hear about people collecting cans and bottles?" she asked. "Homeless people with shopping carts and bags." But it also reminded her of what she was trying to accomplish with her son: If there are a lot of things that he wants, he's going to have to work in order to buy most of them.

Kids Like to Work
(and Why We Don't Let Them)

Many parents echo Aleksandra Gradinarova's questions about their children turning can collecting into a hobby or a part-time job: Isn't redeeming recyclables for money something only poor people do? Shouldn't we leave the cans for them? And if it isn't something we need to do to pay the bills, then why is my child so obsessed with the idea?

Stephanie Preston runs the ecological neuroscience laboratory at the University of Michigan, where they specialize in figuring out how people make decisions about allocating resources. I thought she'd have a developmental or evolutionary answer to these questions about can collection and would tell me all about her work with squirrels and how they store nuts to use later. Instead, she had her own tales of exchanging bottles for dollars. While on a bicycling trip after college, she collected them herself. The $10 she received in return made an appreciable difference in what and how much she could eat each day. Now, she lets her kids buy a little something at the grocery store with the money they get by bringing their own cans and bottles in to reclaim the prepaid deposit.

The explanation for all this can collecting, it turns out, is just basic economic behavior. Kids like to work and enjoy earning money; we just don't do a good enough job of encouraging their industriousness and helping them find new ways to earn. The cans and bottles are part of the proof: Children gravitate to the task because it requires no skill or experience. Anyone of any age who can somehow get to a redemption center can do a little work and make a little money from the refuse immediately at hand. The more kids collect, the more they can earn. Making money makes children feel more grown-up and proves to the adults in their lives that they can do adultlike things at much younger ages than many modern parents realize.

Our job, then, is to stoke that instinct to work and to earn and see just how far their natural-born industriousness takes them. We can give them bigger and better jobs around the house. We can draw lessons from families who live above the family business. We can shuttle them back and forth to their chosen paid pursuit the same way we might if they needed early-morning rides to swim practice five days a week. We can even ask them to take a much bigger role in paying for college than we might have thought possible.

Or we can do none of these things, which is what many of us do reflexively nowadays. Our reluctance to recognize and culti-vate the work ethic in children is rooted in a transformation that occurred relatively recently. We've gone, as Princeton sociologist Viviana A. Zelizer wrote, from celebrating the birth of a child as the "arrival of a future laborer" to a society where "a child is sim-ply not expected to be useful." As kids stopped dying of child-hood diseases, and as families moved off the farm and stopped living together and relying on one another quite so much, kids became worth much less from a purely economic standpoint. As their adolescence has lengthened, we've invested so much more time and money in helping them meet their potential. The title of Zelizer's book—*Pricing the Priceless Child*—both captures the feelings we have about our children and hints at the lengths we'll go to in order to protect them.

No one wants to return to the days when children worked full-time on the farm or in factories at the age of 12. But many parents have swung to the opposite extreme in the past decade or two, shielding even their oldest children at home from paid work altogether. In 1998 about 45 percent of American kids ages 16 to 19 had jobs of some sort, roughly where the number had been for half a century. But not long after, that number fell off a cliff and just kept falling. By 2013, just 20 percent of teens had jobs, an all-time low since the United States started keeping track in 1948.

Why are so few teenagers working these days, when even the youngest kids show such clear signs of industriousness and capability? There are plenty of partial explanations. Many jobs aren't as easy to get as they used to be. Particularly in the late 2000s and early 2010s, lots of adults became willing to take the kinds of jobs that teenagers had typically held, such as those in fast-food restaurants and retail shops. Competing against teens, they usually get the work since they generally have more experience and flexible schedules. Also, as states became stricter about who could drive and at what times of day, it became harder for teens to get to and from many jobs.

But another factor here is a persistent conviction in more affluent and achievement-oriented communities that jobs do damage to kids' college admission prospects. When I ask people whether their high school–aged kids work during the school year, many of them look at me quizzically. The first thing they usually do is express concern about how a job would affect their children's grades.

They needn't be worried. Part-time jobs are correlated with high college expectations and good grade point averages so long as a teenager doesn't work for more than 15 hours or so each week. One of the more thorough studies on the topic noted that parents often forget that there isn't a zero-sum trade-off between working and studying. Teenagers spend plenty of time watching television and hanging out with their friends, so working may not reduce studying time one bit. This is not to say that a part-time job will boost your child's grades, but it does suggest that the right job may not hurt them.

Still, isn't an admissions officer at the college of our children's dreams going to wonder why the kid picked paid work over captaining the debate team or picking up a second team sport? According to Joie Jager-Hyman, a former assistant director of admissions at Dartmouth College who is now a private consultant for college applicants, high school seniors who don't need the money they earn from paid work do indeed have a high bar to clear with many of the people who read their applications. "You need national recognition in some area," she said, ticking off athletics, academics, or charity work as likely sources. The colleges want us to believe this too; when the Massachusetts Institute of Technology put out a news release in late 2013 about its early-admission acceptances, it proudly noted that more than one-third of the incoming students had won some kind of national or international honor.

These sorts of accolades are technically possible in the world of work. There are national barista champions and plenty of competitions for teenage entrepreneurs. Then again, so many of us have promised ourselves that we would avoid spending 15 years of our parenting lives following the prescribed paths that college admissions experts urge us onto. Recognition is nice, but work experience that imparts essential character traits matters plenty.

What our kids can learn from paid employment is a work ethic, that loose phrase that captures the ability to listen, exert ourselves, cooperate with others, do our best, and stick to a task until we've done it, and done it right. Or we could just call it "grit," a term that University of Pennsylvania professor Angela Duckworth has helped popularize in recent years. To her, grit is the answer to this question: Why do some people accomplish more than others who are just as smart as they are? "Grit," she and a colleague wrote in a short essay that appeared in 2013, "is distinguished from the general tendency to be reliable, self-controlled, orderly, and industrious, with its emphasis on long-term stamina rather than short-term intensity." By developing tests of grit, Duckworth has been able to prove that high grit scores predict superior performance on everything from national spelling bees to retention at West Point. It's more predictive, in fact, than IQ tests.

In short, it sounds like just the thing that a part-time job doing relatively menial tasks can teach. And Duckworth fantasizes about putting her own preteen daughters to work. "I would break the law to get my kids a paid job right now," she said. "Where their boss is not their mom. Someone who doesn't give a shit, and you just have to show up and perform." It is not a coincidence, she believes, that all the psychology graduate students who have ended up working at her grit lab at Penn got their first jobs at or below the legal working age.

Better Chores, More of Them, and Sooner

Working at a job before you're of legal age is a bit extreme, even if it may land you in a prestigious Penn lab. So start the job in the home, where we can help our kids act on what Stanford psychologist William Damon describes as a drive for competence. "They avidly seek real responsibility and are gratified when adults give it to them," he wrote in *Greater Expectations*, his book about how far our expectations for our children have sunk in recent decades. Indeed, in many urban and suburban families, the chores that we assign them don't add up to much. It's all too easy to default to the assumption that it's more trouble to teach kids how to perform more complicated household tasks than it is to just do them ourselves, indefinitely. In doing so, however, we send a clear, strong message, according to Damon: We expect little of you, and you're living mostly for yourself.

Every couple of months, someone sends me a link to a particular list of appropriate chores for children of different ages. The chart originates with the Montessori school movement, where children use tools at younger ages than most others do and choose activities that the teachers refer to as work. The chart suggests that 2- and 3-year-olds can carry firewood, that 6- and

7-year-olds should empty the dishwasher, and that 12-year-olds ought to do the grocery shopping. Invariably, the sender includes a note with some version of the general message: If only!

My response is, "Well, why not you? And why not food?" We parents are all in the business of supplying 21 meals a week, plus snacks, so food preparation is probably the biggest household task there is. In late 2013, my family was transfixed by Sarah Lane, a 9-year-old girl who advanced to the final rounds of the reality show *MasterChef Junior*, cooking Beef Wellington and other complicated dishes along the way. She was the youngest contestant, yet it was obvious that she'd been handling knives and cooking over flames for years. Who raised this child? I wondered.

A few calls to the Fox television network yielded the answer: Stephanie Lane, a single mom in Los Angeles, who filled me in on the backstory. Sarah had spent much of her young life in Lancaster, Pennsylvania, where her grandmother owned a restaurant at which Stephanie worked as a waitress. So Sarah had grown up around food; she was wielding a vegetable peeler by age 4. The knives came a year or two later and still make Stephanie a bit nervous. "I will often turn my head," she said, laughing. "But I think there are people who live happy and full lives with nine fingers or fewer, so I'm not that concerned." Sarah knows how to make her mother coffee in the mornings too, and Stephanie certainly doesn't want that to stop.

In Japan, schoolchildren Sarah's age and younger serve and clean up lunch themselves each day. The English translation for the daily ritual is "honorable mealtime," which is meant to convey the seriousness of what might otherwise be a mundane routine. Teachers leave the room at an appointed hour, and the day's designated students don chef's whites and head to the school kitchen. They return carrying giant pots of stew and rice, and they serve their fellow students and lug the empties back to the kitchen.

The scene transfixed T. R. Reid, who wrote a book about the years that he and his wife and children spent living in Japan. "It was an adorable thing to watch, all these tiny creatures, 6, 8, 10 years old, dishing up lunch from tall iron pots in their play-time chef's clothing," he wrote. "Except this wasn't playtime. The school wanted lunch, and it was the students' responsibility to see that it was served." His daughters attended Japanese schools, and one of them told her classmates that in the United States, grown-ups are paid to serve the children meals and clean up after them. Nobody believed her. In national surveys, 75 percent of Japanese children cite working hard as a top priority; 25 percent of American kids do.

Getting our own children to do more, and earlier, in the way of preparing, cooking, and cleaning up after meals isn't easy. It takes practice and persistence, in the same way we may need to hover over them during the first months of music lessons as they whine and complain when things don't come out quite right. Still, failure should not be an option. Every child is capable of contributing to meals in a significant way, and we shouldn't need to pay them to set the table, boil the pasta, or clean it up. It's not as if we lack leverage: We control dessert, first and foremost. But playdates, screen time, and car privileges are all tools we can use if our kids need more than a gentle nudge to finish their regular work around the house and in the kitchen.

What We Can Learn from Farm Families

When children grow up in a family that owns a business, they're likely to start working earlier than kids who have to find strangers to hire them. The labor laws are often less strict when you're working for your own family, as well. Families that literally live on top of their businesses are more likely than most to put their kids to work, due to simple proximity. And within that category, farms offer more opportunities to work than nearly any other business. This is doubly true for dairy farms, where cows need milking and manure needs shoveling on a daily basis.

So one autumn Saturday morning, I drove north from Salt Lake City to Lewiston, Utah, just south of the Idaho border. There, Jackson and Oralie Smith and their seven sons raise 1,800 cows. The boys range in age from 6 to 19, and over the years, their parents have developed a keen sense of the kind of work kids can do and how much of it. Zeb, their 6-year-old, started working at age 5. He washes the nipples for the bottles that the calves drink from and steers the tractor as it creeps up and down the rows of their pens. The next oldest boys participate in or supervise the feedings, while others stack and move giant bales of straw and hay around the property. The older boys also participate in the 4:00 a.m. scraping of the corrals, a euphemism for pushing manure into its proper place and disposing of it. "It sucks," said Zeb, who is old enough to tag along with his older brothers (and mimic their vocabulary) but young enough to take a nap in church on days that he's worked in the morning. The brothers work six days a week, either at the crack of dawn or for two hours after school.

The boys earn no money for keeping their rooms clean or clearing the table. But when it comes to farm work, their parents pay them because they figure that collectively, they do the work of one full-time employee. So each boy gets a proper paper paycheck, which the younger ones often deposit in person at the Lewiston State Bank. They cash it sometimes too and once walked out with a pile of $2 bills. "I do have friends who make them do the work for free, and then they tell their kids that they'll pay for their school clothes and gas," Oralie said. "But some of them ran into situations where the kids begin to resent it."

Starting in sixth grade, the Smith boys make all their own purchasing decisions after a 10 percent tithe to the Mormon church. They receive no money from their parents other than the $500 or so a month they're earning by then. (Zeb started off with a $10 check every two weeks at the age of 5.) While their parents help them make lists of the sorts of school clothes they need, they make their own decisions about what they actually buy from Wrangler. If they want a $160 pair of cowboy boots, they need to figure out how to economize elsewhere.

Their paychecks cover the things they need. In the Wants category, they get a .22 rifle for Christmas at age 12, and at 16 they usually get a shotgun. Still, they swap and sell older items among themselves; Zeb just got his first BB gun and was happily waving it around on the day I visited, trying to shoot the birds that can spread disease to the cows. The boys also buy their own vehicles once they're old enough and purchase horses to train and resell later.

The boys don't have a lot of time for extracurricular activities. One or another of them is usually in the Boy Scouts or wrestling. If so, they'll do their farm work late in the day. But football tryouts come and go without them: The daily practices would cut into their work and interfere with family horseback riding and camping trips at the end of the summer. "We can't put the boys in anything that requires a lot of running around," Oralie said. But she is by no means apologizing. "I have my own ways of teaching them teamwork," she added. "In our town, it's known that, if our boys come, it's going to get done. We move furniture, load hay for the guy whose wife got hurt, and stain decks. They know how to work."

The Smith dairy farm is an oversize operation in almost every way: more cows, more smells, more kids, more activity. But to me the biggest lesson comes from the smallest family member, Zeb. There is a presumption that he will work, that his family members will teach him how, and that he will be good at it, quickly. And while none of the boys is a great scholar or star athlete, their parents operate under the assumption that the ability to perform basic labor is something within every child's grasp. They know that not every boy will grow up to work in the family business, but they're confident that none of them will be afraid of the effort it takes to succeed someplace else.

Facilitating Work: Jet Skis, Suburban Hillbillies, and the Quest for a Horse

Cultivating a work ethic in their children as the Smith family does is not easy for families who don't have paid work readily available. So it may take some extra parental effort to create or supervise such meaningful work or to transport kids to it.

When Len Scarpinato's son, Mark, was in his early teens, Len bought the cheapest house on one of the nicest lakes outside Milwaukee, Wisconsin. Instead of hiring a contractor to fix it up, however, he hired his son. Len is a fix-it guy himself and had taught his son the basics of Sheetrock, painting, demolition, and landscaping. At the lake house, Len would start bigger projects alongside Mark to make sure he understood the task at hand and then leave him on his own to see it through, though he was always a short ride away if his son needed guidance. The payment was a bit more than minimum wage, and it came in the form of "Lake Dollars" that Mark could redeem for all the toys a teenager might want at a lake house. Mark quickly became an expert on used Jet Skis, snowmobiles, and their assorted accessories.

Mark transferred the discipline he learned in improving his construction skills to his work on the football field and in the weight room. Midway through high school, he heard about older teammates who were going to attend college for free, thanks to athletic scholarships. When his parents offered to use their college savings for graduate school if he could earn an undergraduate athletic scholarship, he didn't just train harder. He spent hundreds of dollars of his own money on a consultant to help package himself better. On January 1, 2014, he helped anchor the Michigan State defense, and he and his teammates won the Rose Bowl.

There is no end to the potential costs for youth sports, and some parents reach their limit sooner than others. Mark Scarpinato chipped in for his college scholarship consultant, but he was lucky enough to have fallen in love with a sport that did not involve expensive travel teams.

His story contrasts with that of 14-year-old Cali Drouillard, whose parents could never cover all the expenses she runs up pursuing what may be the most expensive sport of all: showing horses. Her mother, Andrea, works as a sales manager; her father suffers from multiple sclerosis and cannot work. Giving up the sport and her goal to own a horse is a theoretical option, but the experiences will help her meet her goal of pursuing a career in the veterinary sciences. She has her eye on an undergraduate program in that field at Oklahoma State, even though she comes from Bloomfield Hills, Michigan. Cali has a friend who jokes that she's the only country girl in the Detroit suburbs and refers to her as the Bloomfield hillbilly.

But a hillbilly in the suburbs needs earning power, especially if her family is not among the wealthiest in an otherwise affluent community. The Drouillards do not live in one of the more expensive neighborhoods. They make their mortgage payments without too much trouble, but they could never afford the $50,000 initiation fee at the fanciest riding facility in the area. Cali rides at an open-to-all farm nearby, and she's fine with that. Still, her sport requires the use of a large, live animal, and her goal to have her own horse comes with an especially long list of costs. So her quest began with knowing every one of them, starting with what a horse needs to eat each week. She's listed each item on a spreadsheet. First, there's the $2,500 to $5,000 to buy the type of horse she wants. Then there's the horse's basic room and board, which doesn't include medicine or visits to the veterinarian. Saddles, bridles, and horseshoes come next. That's before the lessons start, and there are additional costs if she wants to travel with the horse to competitions. Cali can tick them all off from memory now, and she haunts various Facebook pages where used equipment goes up for sale.

As Cali grew increasingly fond of the sport, the bills added up. "I told her she could raise chickens or turkey or livestock," Andrea said. "But I couldn't continue to be her sugar mama." Having issued the challenge, Andrea eventually had to decide how far she was willing to go, literally, to help her daughter respond to it. Not long after, Cali spoke to a friend whose uncle had a farm with 1,000 head of cattle a few hours north of where Cali lives. The friend had cut a deal with her uncle, who allowed her to help raise a steer in exchange for a portion of the sale price. She offered to get Cali in on the deal and Andrea quickly traded in her car for a Chevy Volt with sky-high mileage so she could ferry Cali up to the farm.

The logistics proved too complicated, however, so Cali started babysitting, pet sitting, and putting away any and all birthday and Christmas presents to put toward her sport. "I need the money for paying my mom back," she explained. "Up until this year, I hadn't understood how much it cost to ride horses. Now I think of this as kind of a game. The more time I put in, the more money I end up getting. I love raising animals, and it's what I want to do for the rest of my life."

Families that can pay for every athletic pursuit, no matter the cost, shouldn't let their kids off easy either. Joline Godfrey, the consultant who works with wealthy families, encourages them to ask their kids to take on extra chores. Older kids might tackle the planning, for instance: tracking the swim practice and meet schedule, sending weekly memos to the parent who does the driving, booking the hotel rooms, and creating family itineraries for when the soccer travel team goes on the road. "If you're withholding all that responsibility, kids get all the privileges with none of the opportunity to build capacity," she said. "And that's what we're talking about here, building capacity for children."

They Can Pay for Some of College, Too

Michael Winerip and his wife, Sandy Keenan, worried about their children's capacity for hard work. Their four kids grew up with more advantages than they had had themselves. And while the pair, who live on Long Island and are journalist colleagues of mine, were willing to pay for most college expenses, they wanted to teach their kids to find a job and stick to it. So they settled on a plan, a stretch target for each of their kids: Every one of them would pay for the first semester of college tuition themselves. To do this, they would need as much as $15,000 each. "The idea of having them pay for a semester isn't the big thought," explained Winerip. "It's implanting a work ethic at a very young age that's crucial."

Keenan had started working in ninth grade, giving tennis lessons to younger children. Winerip had began even earlier, at age 11. At 6 in the morning he sold newspapers at a factory, where the Boston Gear Works employees would give him a dime for an 8-cent paper and let him and his younger brother keep the change. But he was able to do the job only because his mother got him up at 5:30 in the morning so he could ride his bicycle to work. "She was a Depression-era kid who had lived in a tenement," he said. "She had those values. I was 11 years old, and I wasn't going to do it on my own."

He has tried to follow her example as a parent. When his oldest child was in sixth grade, he got the boy up at 5:30 a.m. so he could walk over to the local deli to put the Sunday newspapers together. His son hung on to that gig until he could get a better job. As year-round residents of a beach community on Long Island, the children had opportunities to meet the high demand for seasonal labor. As younger teens, they got jobs cleaning toilets at the beach in the morning, and their parents would drive them over in the early morning. Then the teens would sell ice cream in the afternoon and umpire games for younger kids. Eventually, all four of them worked as lifeguards, which allowed them to earn more than $8,000 during many summers.

The kids, who all knew about the first-semester-tuition requirement years in advance, bellyached a little bit. "There were times when they'd come home and complain that their supervisor was a jerk," Winerip recalled. "And we'd explain that that's why you have to go to college." He and his wife also hoped that the kids would remember the hundreds of hours in the lifeguard chair and the untold number of toilets they'd scrubbed to collect that $15,000 when they were tempted to blow off class during their freshman year. That worked with all but one of the kids. One son dropped out, came home, and rebooted in community college, where he eventually earned a partial scholarship to attend New York University.

The pay-your-tuition gambit may seem like an extreme parenting move, but it's really just a return to what we once saw as normal. A generation ago, many college students worked their way through school. While it's almost impossible for college students to do that today, letting them attend without asking anything of them financially may actually be damaging. A 2013 study found that the higher the percentage that parents contribute to a child's college costs, the worse their grades tend to be, though the correlations aren't quite as strong at highly competitive schools. Still, having some financial skin in the game seems to matter.

Winerip smirked when I asked him whether he thinks college admissions officers looked askance at his kids' decision to work during the summer instead of doing something more intellectually or globally prestigious. "The kids who go to Costa Rica for the summer to do volunteer work are a dime a dozen," he said. As the number of teens engaged in paid work continues to fall, it's kids like his that may start to stand out more.

Cans, Bottles, and the Big Payoff

Plenty of children will never know what it means to truly need to work. Parents can't explain what it feels like, even if they had to do it themselves. Still, these kids who must work or don't have much money to spare are among us, if not at our community schools then at most of the colleges our kids will someday attend. And for these children, work can be transformative. Their stories about it can, all by themselves, help pull other kids out of their own lives and imagine what it might be like to come from very different circumstances.

The story I tell my own daughter is about Lucerito Gutierrez, her two older sisters, and their mother. Fifteen years ago, they sold their mother's tamales on the streets of San Diego to make ends meet. Lucerito's single mother was a housekeeper by day, but her earnings weren't enough to pay for the three girls' expenses. After a few years of selling tamales in parks, her mother began to notice all the discarded cans and bottles there, and realized that, with her small team of collectors, they could make the same money or more in much less time by filling bags and carts and taking them to the recycling center. The Gutierrezes were not able to afford a car until a few years ago, so they usually pushed and pulled their haul 90 minutes each way.

The family followed a fairly precise routine. They wore gloves to avoid cuts and close-fitting pants for getting into dumpsters, plus long-sleeve shirts for reaching into garbage cans, no matter the weather. An animal check preceded each pickup. "You try to kick the garbage can to make a sound or throw a rock," Lucerito said, recalling the rats and raccoons she'd unexpectedly roused in the past. "You don't put your hands in first. You use a stick to move stuff around."

Despite the hazards, the family made just enough money that, together with what they collected in public assistance, they could move from a one-room garage to an actual apartment, though in a dangerous neighborhood; they later moved to the small rental house on a quiet street where they live now. Some months are better than others. There have been weeks when the family ate mostly rice and beans and others where they have enough money from the cans and bottles to treat themselves to 49-cent burgers at Carl's Jr.

By the time Lucerito was in middle school, she was getting tired of earning money through her family's collecting. "I knew I didn't want to live like that for the rest of my life," she said. Her middle school offered an engineering course, and while she had no idea what it was, she took the class and got hooked. Her teacher took an interest in her, and she entered a mentorship program where she met college professors.

One day, while attending an after-school class, she learned about a San Diego nonprofit organization called Reality Changers. The program selects high-potential, low-income high school students who would be the first in their families to attend college. Then, it puts them through an intensive curriculum to get them ready for standardized tests and college applications. Among other requirements, parents of participating students must cook dinner for the other students at least once each term. Lucerito's mother made the tamales they once sold in the park.

During her senior year, with help from her tutors at Reality Changers, Lucerito was accepted into the engineering program at the University of California, San Diego. Then, she summoned her courage and shot for the moon: a scholarship from the Gates Foundation. "What most of my high-school classmates do not know is that, even though I am taking four Advanced Placement classes this year, I still go dumpster diving with my mother four days a week," she wrote in her application essay. "I want to use my scholarship at UCSD to become an engineer who will revolutionize the way societal roadblocks are perceived."

In the spring of 2013, she heard back from the foundation, and it informed her that she had won a Gates Millennium scholarship. The foundation will cover up to $300,000 in tuition and other costs for her undergraduate and graduate education. That's about five times more than Lucerito's family collected in over a decade of gathering cans and bottles on the streets of San Diego.

8

The Luckiest

Instilling gratitude, grace, and perspective
in our sons and daughters

In the summer of 2012, comedian Chris Rock was a guest on *The Daily Show with Jon Stewart*. Fathers both, they had gotten to talking about Rock's various projects, and Stewart questioned whether Rock's heavy workload was merely a convenient way to avoid spending time with his family. Rock admitted it, and the audience began to chuckle. But then he and Stewart launched into an extended riff on the uncomfortable truths about raising children, repeatedly slapping the table in front of them for emphasis while the crowd egged them on, laughing uproariously.

ROCK: I just do not like these people. I don't understand them. My kids are rich, I have nothing in common with them.

STEWART: How do you explain this to them? I'm trying to
figure this out. I had jobs since I was 14 ... I don't know
how to explain it to them. . . . It's a different world.
Maybe there should be like an Outward Bound that we
put them in where it's like "you've got to live like shit for
a week."

ROCK: Every summer I beg my wife to put 'em in camp
in Harlem, and she won't do it. I think my whole rich-
ass neighborhood needs to go to camp in Harlem in
the summer and get their lunch money taken and [get]
beat up. . . . There's gotta be a Camp Kick-Ass!

STEWART: I think that's an excellent idea. You should
franchise that.

This was a genius bit of comedy; we don't need to be as well
off as Rock and Stewart to identify with much of what they're
saying. They don't come right out and call their children spoiled.
That would be cruel, it may not be true, and it certainly wouldn't
be funny. Instead, it's the word *rich* that comes up first, and
Rock tags his kids with the adjective while explicitly refusing to
place himself in this group. It quickly becomes clear that both
these fathers are operating in unfamiliar territory, given one's
upbringing in Harlem and the other's in a town where lots of
teens had part-time jobs. They are so unnerved by their good
fortune, in fact, that Stewart can't figure out how to communicate his family's privilege to his children and Rock can't agree
on a course of action with his spouse. The necessary solution,
however, is crystal clear to both of them: Camp Kick-Ass. Not a
literal butt kicking but a new perspective.

And so it is with many of us. We may not be in the same

category of wealth, but many of us have enough to give our kids everything they need and much of what they want. And even if we have less than many people we know in our communities, we have more than most in our country and our world. We know this, but our kids probably don't quite yet. So how do we make them aware of just how good they have it, without preaching to them or making them pity others who have less? And how do we remove them from their life of relative ease every so often and expose them to people and places that are not like the ones in their everyday lives?

I've heard two reflexive responses to these questions over the years. The first goes something like this: Do you know how privileged you sound even asking those questions? I do. Part of the point of the exercise here is to recognize whatever privileges we have and acknowledge that it's a luxury to be the person asking the questions. The second response is that the solution is easy; families should simply move to a more diverse community and put their kids in schools with students from families with many different incomes. It's a fine idea, but it's unrealistic to expect that most people will do this. Plenty of parents do whatever they can to enroll their children in the most high-achieving schools, wherever they are. Treating that act of devotion like some kind of character flaw is unfair. Yes, it's true that many of the communities that have those great schools lack much socioeconomic diversity, and plenty of private schools are less inclusive than they could be. But even at highly diverse public schools with excellent test scores, plenty of self-segregation goes on among the students and parents. The perfect community is ever elusive, so almost all of us need to be doing more to help our children understand how much they have and where they fit in.

Why We're Confused About Class

When I bring up the topic of social class with parents, many of them visibly squirm. Beyond our general tendency to avoid conversations about money, it can be difficult to step back and recognize our own good fortune. Context explains some of it. It can be uncomfortable to have lots of friends who have much more or less money than we do, so we tend to hang around people who are more like ourselves. Once we make that choice, some of our peers will probably seem wealthier than we are, while others will appear to have somewhat less. That leaves us in the middle, where it becomes very easy to default into assuming that we're middle class.

In the United States, people in the middle have a household income of about $50,000. So anyone who has a household income that is two to four times that is not middle class, even if they've chosen to live in an area with a cost of living that is higher than average. People get confused about this in more affluent suburbs and most private school communities, where there are almost always people who have more or spend more. They must be the rich ones, right? In New York, it's the bankers. In Los Angeles, it's the A-list producers and directors and actors. In San Francisco, it's the technology people. And everywhere, it's the surgeons and the law firm partners and the people with family businesses or inherited money. As long as there are people who have more, everyone else talks as if they're middle class and claims not to be among the truly privileged.

Many people reading this book, however, are decidedly upper class. Above about $75,000 in household income, we graduate into the top third of income in the United States. Euphemisms abound in this category, since those who earn this much may not feel anywhere close to rich. So they are "upper middle class" or "upper income" or "affluent." These terms don't capture the basic facts though: Almost all of us who have landed in that upper third don't truly *need* much more of the things that money can buy. Responding to our cravings for those additional *wants* on the margin is a lifelong task for adults, but we've got only 20 years or so to raise kids who know how good they have it.

Many parents avoid talking to their kids about socioeconomic status because they believe that children don't notice class differences until they're teenagers. But very young children have a basic sense of what the words *rich* and *poor* mean. In a research study conducted by Patricia G. Ramsey, a psychology professor at Mount Holyoke College, she showed 3-year-olds a series of photographs and distinguished between the haves and have-nots. Only half of her subjects thought that the rich and poor people in the pictures would be friends with one another. Other research has shown that 6-year-olds keep score of which kids have what sorts of possessions and begin to make judgments accordingly. By 11 or so, they're beginning to assume that social class is related to ambition. Around age 14, they begin to wonder whether there is a larger economic system at work that may constrain movement between classes. So even as we're sorting out our own complicated feelings about the smaller differences between ourselves and many of the people we know, kids are jumping to even bigger conclusions about larger differences. They may not come to the right ones—or to more nuanced ones—if we're not engaging them in conversation all along the way.

This ongoing discussion is particularly important when it comes to social media. When kids first start interacting with one another online, it's mostly jokes and innocent flirting. They're among friends, after all—people they have chosen to communicate with and whose online invitations they have accepted. But what teenagers miss is that many of their peers use social media to sell the best version of themselves, whether they're doing it consciously or not. They post the most attractive pictures. The nicest clothing they own. The parties and vacations and events that not everyone can go to. I have lost count of the number of disgusted parents who have complained to me about their kids following Michael Dell's kids on Instagram or others who were posting photos of themselves on private jets. What began as a way to extend and maintain relationships has become, in part, a vast vista of jealousy and one-upmanship.

Not every child will suffer from this exposure. But it still makes sense to supervise the viewing of social media the same way we do television commercials, at least at first. It's fine to ask kids for their log-in information so we can see what they're seeing. Parents who don't want to go that far can at least sit down and view the feeds alongside their kids for a while, offering commentary on why their friends may be posting what they're posting and whether their own posts may be making others feel left out or left behind.

Gratitude and Grace: Reviving a Family Ritual

Feeling fortunate is good for kids. A number of scholars who are part of a boom in happiness studies have measured gratitude levels in children and found strong correlations between gratitude and higher grades, levels of life satisfaction, and social integration. There's also a link between gratitude and lower levels of envy and depression. In a series of experimental "gratitude interventions," researchers have asked children to keep a gratitude journal or write a letter to someone who has had a lasting impact on them and then read the letter aloud to that person. These activities made kids feel more optimistic.

So how best to foster a culture of family gratitude without having it become a chore or feeling rote? One way is to establish a grace-saying ritual. Nearly 3,000 years ago, Homer wrote that no one would "dare to drink till he had made libation to the Zeus All-Mighty." Deuteronomy 8:10 commands all who have finished eating to "praise the Lord your God for the good land he has given you." An Egyptian inscription from about 150 BC offers up prayer to the table god for pharaohs to say before eating meat.

Modern Americans appear to be less thankful for the intervention of any particular god. Just 44 percent of them report saying daily grace or a similar blessing before meals, while 46 percent claim rarely to say it at all. But if discomfort with the idea of a divine spirit is what's keeping us from expressing gratitude, then we need to find ways to say a godless grace. It can be as simple as asking everyone at the table to talk about one thing that happened that day that made them feel grateful or lucky. Or if that feels too formal, ask everyone to make a toast to someone they encountered that day. Or take turns making just one each night.

If we're going to start a national grace-saying movement, it needs to be flexible. Even one word can go a long way. Lisa

Cepeda and Antonio Cepeda-Benito are among the very few parents who always manage miraculously to gather their kids for breakfast and dinner each day, and they began a special tradition about 20 years ago. Their son Agustín was in kindergarten in Indiana, and he came home and told his parents that they had said a small prayer before eating lunch. The pair had never been much for attending formal worship services. Still, they decided that to honor Agustín's wish to bless the family meal at home, they would simply say thank you. Since the family speaks Spanish at home, they decided to do it in that language.

On the night I visited them in South Burlington, Vermont, where they now live, they served salad and homemade pizza and oversize chocolate chip cookies. But before we got to eat any of that, we all clasped hands, closed our eyes, bowed our heads and uttered one word: *gracias*. Then Lisa, who is a psychologist, and Antonio, who is dean of the College of Arts and Sciences at the University of Vermont, explained why they keep the ritual going:

> LISA: If we don't do it now, it feels unsettled.
> ANTONIO: It's a reminder that we are a family and that we are together.
> LISA: Though we're not always holding hands.
> ANTONIO: It does many good things. If we have an argument . . .
> LISA: If we're upset, we just do a fist bump, and all the kids know . . .
> ANTONIO: But it gets you closer to making up! If feelings got hurt, it reduces the sharpness through human contact.

Part of the beauty of the gesture is that it is an empty vessel, one that all the people around the table fill with their own meaning on that day, in that single moment of silence. *Gracias.*

Another regularly scheduled bit of gratitude that might interest older kids comes from a documentary called *365 Grateful,* which you can show your children online. In an effort to beat back depression, the filmmaker took one picture each day of something she felt grateful for. Something like this could be a requirement for middle school kids who are begging for their first smartphone. Christine Carter, a sociologist who directs the Greater Good Science Center's parenting program, suggests another possibility for families with older children: Let them invent a new gratitude ritual for the family to adopt. If the kids oversee it, it may feel less like some kind of daily chore.

Gaining Perspective: Teammates, Playdates, and Field Trips

Once we've done what we can to create an environment in our homes that nurtures gratitude and perspective, we can turn to the world outside. Some of us live in socioeconomically diverse neighborhoods, where it's normal to encounter people with a variety of incomes and backgrounds. But many people pick their communities for the quality of the public schools, and often these "not-so-public" schools, as sociologist Allison Pugh describes them, aren't so economically diverse. If the schools are great, home prices spiral ever higher and the communities become filled with people who have enough money to pay the entry fee.

So if we want our children to be more sensitive to the fact that not everyone has what they have, it helps to seek out cross-class friendships, both for our kids and for ourselves. Any effort to forge those relationships, however, creates uncomfortable questions. Why try at all? The point can't be simply to teach children what it would be like if their own family had less money. No family wants to be the source of a child's edification. Nor should families with less be objects of pity.

Heather Johnson, a mother of three in Bethlehem, Pennsylvania, has spent many years coming up with a better answer. Johnson, her husband, and their daughter are white; their twin sons, whom they adopted from Haiti, are black. The boys play on a Little League team where they are the only players who are not from working-class or poor Dominican or Puerto Rican families. The Johnsons try to blend in as best they can, leaving their Nikon camera at home and attending the $7 all-you-can-eat pancake fund-raiser at Applebee's without suggesting that the campaign aim higher. At both practices and games, which every member of every family is expected to attend, Johnson is the only mother who speaks English as a first language. "It is awkward," she said. "There is a lot of sitting on my hands with the other moms. There was a day when my daughter brought blueberries, and they wanted to let their kids try them because they had never had them before."

When she's not at the baseball field, Johnson is a sociology professor at Lehigh University who focuses her research on social class and the perpetuation of wealth and poverty. She believes that many kids have settled into an understanding of social class as something you earn through merit and hard work—and that you don't deserve to be in the highest socioeconomic classes if you don't work hard enough. Plenty of parents and teachers are fine with that, since it dovetails nicely with the desire to get children to buckle down in school and is conveniently compatible with the persistent idea that all kids in America have an equal opportunity to make something of themselves.

But Johnson doesn't quite buy the idea of a pure meritocracy, and it can make people nervous when she explains it out loud. "There is often more to the story than just hard work," she explained during a talk to teachers at the Gordon School in Providence, Rhode Island. "It's not *but*. It's *and*. There is luck and circumstance and the family you were born to. All sorts of things factor in. That would be extremely radical if parents just started saying *that* at the dinner table. If we were honest about our own privilege when we have it. And not all of us have it or have had it, though most of us in this room have had it in some form or another."

And so it is with her family, having adopted Haitian sons and being able to send them to private school while many of their baseball teammates were born into immigrant families where no one has gone to college. They may play together now, but it will be harder for many of them to find their way to college teams than it may be for Johnson's sons. This is not because they are better players, and it's important to her that her boys come to understand this and why it's not very fair.

The lessons need not always be quite as heavy as this. One good reason for kids to hang out with people who are different from them is to realize that nobody has a monopoly on happiness and that it's often great fun to slip into a world that is not like your own. Team sports are just one way to bridge this gap. Citywide choruses and countywide orchestras often include children from across the class spectrum. For older kids who have forged cross-class relationships on their own, offer to have the friend's whole family over for a meal. Having less or more than everyone else in a classroom or a community can be confusing for a kid and complicated for a parent. But as long as a gesture is genuine, other families will probably see it in that light.

The daughter of Sotha Saing, the San Francisco mother who came to the United States as a Cambodian refugee and is adamant about her kids' working for their allowance, once received an invitation to sleep over at a friend's home in an affluent neighborhood. "It was a family I didn't know, and she gave me the address, and I knew it was going to be a whole bunch of questions," she said. "But I want her to grow and see everything, and not shelter my child."

Her daughter was quiet when she first returned the next day, but soon enough the observations and inquiries poured forth. The enormous room that the friend had all to herself. All the latest video games. The questions about what her parents did for a living to afford all of that. Saing explained to her daughter that she did not know the answers. "But I explained that there were a couple of ways they could have gotten that house," she said. "Her parents may have worked hard to get it. But they could have inherited it or the money to buy it." That opened the door for Saing to remind her daughter that she had a mother who wasn't born in the United States, and that she was trying to lay down a path for her daughter to succeed. Saing was even trying to buy some life insurance so her daughter could inherit money too someday. "There was a little bit of sadness," Saing said. "But she had fun. And I told her that if she liked all those things, maybe she could sleep over there more often so we didn't have to buy them! Her friend can't play with them all by herself."

At Manhattan Country School in New York City, the pre-kindergarten teachers believe that teaching students how their classmates live is important enough that they take field trips to one another's homes. The kindergarten-through-eighth-grade school sets tuition on an income-based sliding scale; the truly wealthy pay a bit more than they would at comparable schools but about 70 percent of the families pay less than the maximum. The home visits began a couple of decades ago, when an Indian-American boy approached one of the teachers expressing frustration that his peers thought he used tomahawks and wore feathers. A teacher asked if he wanted to invite them over for a visit, and he was thrilled. His mother wore her sari, the kids ate Indian snacks, and they listened to traditional Indian music. It worked so well that the school decided that every one of the 4- and 5-year-olds ought to host a field trip to their homes each year.

Today, the keeper of the tradition is a teacher named Sarah Leibowits. She's been leading the trips for a decade and is also a parent at the school, paying a reduced tuition herself. Students set out in packs of five, armed with worksheets for them to draw pictures of the things they see that excite them. Over the years, the kids have been to housing projects in the Bronx and town houses in some of the most expensive neighborhoods in Manhattan. They travel as their classmates travel each day, tracing whatever the normal bus or subway or walking itinerary is. A parent of the host family is always present, and they serve a snack of the host child's choosing. The food is often a highlight of the trip, along with a full inventorying of the child's toys and other special objects. The host also gives a tour of the neighborhood, pointing out places where the family shops and plays. On the first trip that I tagged along for, one boy took his classmates to visit the African market across the street from his apartment building in Harlem. On the next, the children visited the fountain at Columbia University.

The school's founder, Gus Trowbridge, always thought that the home visit lesson plan was among the most radical pieces of curriculum that he had ever encountered. But as Leibowits has watched it all play out over her years of teaching, she's concluded that the impact on these 4- and 5-year-old kids is fairly subtle. "Children are just really excited to be learning about their friends and finding commonalities," she said. There was no confusion about why so many family members seemed to be living in a one-bedroom apartment in a housing project several years back, and an enormous Central Park South apartment was notable mostly because the children were able to look down at the street and count the horse-drawn carriages.

The visits are mandatory, and every so often a parent causes trouble. It's not the less affluent parents, however, who protest out of shame or a desire for privacy. Several years ago, a parent who was also an alumna of the school wanted a list of every apartment her child was visiting along with its address. When the mother found out that her child was going to a neighborhood that was right on the border of Manhattan and the Bronx, she called the host mother to ask if the neighborhood was safe. A different teacher, herself an alumna of the school, called the inquiring parent and "gave it to her," as Leibowits recalled, saying

"How dare you, as an alumna of the school, do something like this?" The visit went off as planned, and no one suffered any harm on the mean streets of upper Manhattan.

As far as Leibowits knows, no other school has ever copied the home visit curriculum. She wonders whether it might be related to the fact that so many communities and schools are so socioeconomically homogeneous that the kids wouldn't learn anything. Still, most communities have at least some of this diversity, so almost everyone should eventually have an opportunity to host or go on a similar playdate. If not, we can seek out friends or family members out of town who may live differently than we do.

Gaining Perspective:
Helping Others Nearby

Many parents believe that their kids will learn how lucky they are by doing volunteer work, and community service is indeed worth doing for plenty of reasons. Volunteers enable all sorts of service organizations to help larger numbers of people than they could otherwise. But while tutoring, working in a soup kitchen, or participating in neighborhood cleanups are all fine ways to help others, they usually don't help kids develop meaningful and lasting relationships with other kids their age whom they might not otherwise meet.

Lucy Gilchrist, a mother of two in Cleveland, found a different way to include her two daughters in volunteer work that forged a deeper connection. Through her church, she became a volunteer driver for fellow parishioners. While that may not sound like much of a way to help, not having a car makes life extraordinarily complicated in plenty of parts of the country. Many neighborhoods in Cleveland have no decent grocery store, and if you have a new baby, it's hard to take the bus back and forth to a good one.

Gilchrist helped a family that was trying to move out of government-subsidized housing but didn't have any way to travel around the city to see the available rentals. She and her two kids spent many hours driving the other family around in their minivan over two or three days. The two families bonded over their joint attempt to sleuth out various flaws in the rental houses and all the defects that the landlords were trying to hide. "In one of them, the back door was boarded shut, so there was no way you could get out of the kitchen," Gilchrist said. "My kids know what it looks like to have a basement leak, and they were able to point out water when it was down there and when things were broken." Only one of the houses they toured was habitable, and by the end, Gilchrist's kids were helping point out when the landlords were flat-out lying.

Other families in their church have driven a family of Eritrean refugees around the city until they were settled and had their own transportation. "You take them grocery shopping and clothes shopping, and your own kids get a sense of the world that the other families are living in and the decisions they're having to make without its being 'Oh, look at those poor people,'" Gilchrist said. The family that she and her kids helped has since moved again, but the kids still worship in church together and their mothers are now good friends.

The Case Against Volunteer Trips
to Developing Countries

I first heard from Gilchrist because her family's experience in Cleveland made her think there was no reason for kids to take expensive service trips abroad. She contacted me in response to a post I'd written for *The New York Times' Motherlode* blog about a 21-year-old woman named Pippa Biddle, a veteran of many such journeys. Not only had she traveled with her boarding school classmates to volunteer at an orphanage in Africa, she and her family had taken numerous trips to the Dominican Republic to help start a camp for children who are HIV positive. But Biddle was done with what's come to be known as voluntourism, and I featured her on the blog because a post that she had written to explain her point of view had gone viral, reaching millions of people.

Her essay had hit hardest with parents, many of whom don't think carefully enough about the purpose of such trips. Some mothers and fathers pay thousands of dollars to send their kids on volunteer trips because they think it will infuse them with gratitude for all that they have back at home. Others do it because they mistakenly think that this sort of service work is meaningful to college admissions officers at selective schools. (In fact, admissions officers often roll their eyes at the hundreds of application essays that arrive each year from students who have written about these trips.)

Biddle wanted parents to think about what their children were actually qualified to do—the actual work on the ground.

Here's what she wrote about her trip to Africa with her class-mates: "Turns out that we, a group of highly educated private boarding school students, were so bad at the most basic construction work that each night, the men had to take down the structurally unsound bricks we had laid and rebuild the structure so that, when we woke up in the morning, we would be unaware of our failure. It is likely that this was a daily ritual." She concluded that the group could have done a lot more good by taking the money they spent on the trip and hiring qualified local people to build the structure.

She also turns the lens on her own family's work in the Dominican Republic. Volunteers who don't speak fluent Spanish can be more of a burden than a help, given the need to communicate with and care for sick children. This became doubly so when she became sick herself, and the health workers needed to worry about her in addition to the children. Now, she raises money for the project but doesn't visit herself. "I have stopped attending," she wrote, "having finally accepted that my presence there is not the godsend that I was coached by nonprofits, documentaries and service programs to believe it would be."

I asked Pippa's father, Ed Biddle, for his take, and he isn't ready to write off all such trips for all teens. He encourages parents to consider four things. First, who are the leaders? If they are real grown-ups with expertise in the region, then there might be some educational value to the program. Second, does the work to be done leverage the skills of the participants? And if they don't have any skills, how exactly will they be helping? Third, he suggests taking a careful look at how the program is being sold, and by whom. Is it a for-profit operation marketing the beauty of the region or an organization that focuses mostly on the needs of a community and how to help? Finally, he would never send a child on a trip like this with a friend, since preformed cliques can prevent kids from learning from one another.

Pippa thinks her father's list is pretty good, but she would add similar questions to the one that Lucy Gilchrist raised when she first wrote to me: What are your goals, and can you meet them in some other way than by spending a lot of money doing work far away?

How Overnight Camp Can Help

Parents who send older children away for part of the summer may have an additional goal in mind, though we may not always have a name for it. Volunteer trips often begin with the goal of pushing teenagers *toward* something—empathy for others, perspective on their own lives, or a better understanding of the world. But others among us want our kids to get *away* from some of what surrounds them during the school year. We live in the safest communities we can and send our kids to the best possible schools, but these places often come with social pressure to buy and to have things. That environment can give children a warped sense of what they really need in order to thrive and be happy.

Sociologist Allison Pugh refers to the tactics a parent might employ in seeking a more meaningful summer experience as "symbolic deprivation." The symbolism here refers to the fact that there is only so much that most of us are realistically going to change about whatever lives we've set up for our families. And in the context of sleepaway camp, this isn't Chris Rock's vision of Camp Kick-Ass. The deprivation isn't so much about keeping children away from kids who are exactly like them or exposing them to those who are much different. Instead, it's about reminding them that they don't need air-conditioning, travel teams, electronic gadgets, or even electricity to enjoy themselves. In fact, the camps that have few to none of those amenities may provide some of the best perspective of all.

It's not easy to find an overnight camp like this, given the trend in recent years toward ever-bigger water toys and spring-floored gymnastics studios and go-karts and horse-jumping rings and organic food in the no-longer-so-much mess halls. But there are a few holdouts, albeit ones that charge $1,250 per week for the privilege. At the end of a dirt road in a town called Belgrade, Maine, just over an hour northwest of Portland, sits a tiny house and a small dock. A counselor sits behind the wheel of a motorboat that serves as a kind of shuttle bus to a 3-acre island a short trip away. And it is there that Pine Island Camp has hosted no more than 90 boys for at least six weeks during the summer since 1902.

The boys sleep in open-sided tents. There is no electricity, save what powers a few appliances in the dining hall. Bathing happens with biodegradable soap in the lake, naked for all the passing boaters to see. (They have learned to avert their eyes over the years.) The only bathroom is an elevated perch; you climb up a set of stairs, open a screen door and see as many as three boys (or their counselors) sitting on a single wooden board no more than 15 feet wide. The board has three holes, and a composting toilet sits below. A giant window opens up to the lake and its various boats and birds. Campers call it a loo with a view, and it's certainly scenic; they also seem used to visitors popping their heads in just to lay eyes on it. When much of the island burned in 1995, donations poured in from families and alumni, and the rebuilding left things much as they had been except for that new bit of electricity. "I've had people step ashore and, not having been here for 60 years, be kind of stunned," said the camp's director, Ben Swan, after a group of his older campers showed me around one day. "It's essentially the same place. I don't think there's anywhere else in their life where that is likely to be true."

There are no team sports on a day-to-day basis at Pine Island. Swan's father, who bought the camp in 1946 with his two brothers, was a non-jock who almost got kicked out of the University of Virginia for protesting that it had built a mammoth football stadium before it had a decent library. Instead, the emphasis is on activities like canoeing, swimming, and other skills necessary to get the most out of the camping trips that the boys eventually take. Nighttime entertainment comes courtesy of the campers and whatever games and skits they invent. One Pine Island maxim is "re-creation, not recreation," which reflects a desire to send boys home with a lot more confidence and much more awareness of others. "One of the things most valuable about this place, because there isn't much here, is something that I think a vast number of elite colleges have lost," Swan told me while overlooking the lake. "Everyone here is needed to make it work. And that's a huge gift to these kids. There's nothing here! The games are the games that they make up. When everything is all set up for you and your dorm room looks like the Ritz, you won't have to decorate it or maybe they won't even let you."

Then, he got a twinkle in his eye, thinking about the kinds of affluent communities where his campers tend to reside in the off-season. "Who is needed in New Canaan, Connecticut?" he said. "Nobody! They don't need you."

Pine Island Camp is practically singular, but for comparison I visited Birch Rock Camp, another Maine institution that's well known for being the kind of place you seek out when you want to provide an antidote to whatever it is that's surrounding your boys during the school year. It's off a paved road, not a dirt one. The baseball diamond on some leased farmland at the turnoff provides evidence of at least a bit of competition, though the infield is uneven and it lacks much of a right field.

But then I parked my car on a patch of grass and walked down a steep hill to Lake McWain, following clumps of boys and a few adults who were there for an alumni lunch. On the waterfront, all the campers were gathered in their maroon T-shirts keeping an eye on a speck in the water that was slowly coming closer. Birch Rock boys are serious swimmers, and each summer they attempt a long-distance swim. The younger boys begin with a summer of training to complete the Duck, a half-mile across, and then the Loon, out and back, and so on. Only when you are among the oldest boys can you sign up for the Whale, a lap around the lake of more than five miles. All summer, these older boys are in training, and starting two weeks before the end of the camp, they begin taking their shot at it.

As the speck grew near that day, a buzz rose and then, in unison, a chant as the aspiring Whaler came closer stroke by stroke.

"I BELIEVE THAT GABE CAN SWIM!"
"I BELIEVE THAT GABE CAN SWIM!"
"I BELIEVE THAT GABE CAN SWIM!"
"I BELIEVE THAT GABE CAN SWIM!"

I did not know Gabe and had yet to meet a single person at the camp, but I found myself holding back tears. The cheers grew to roars as Gabe reached the dock, followed by his spotter in a canoe. Before he even had a chance to break his stroke, his counselors pulled him in in a single fluid motion, onto the dock, and into a cocoon of blankets. From there, he stumbled slowly up a walkway through a gauntlet of screaming, backslapping fellow campers so he could be whisked off to the nurse, who would check him over for hypothermia.

The Whale, I later learned, is the moment that Birch Rock boys anticipate for years, and it doesn't require a water-ski boat or a stable of horses and fancy riding gear. "We don't think about stuff, we think about soul," said Rich Deering, the camp's alumni and community director. "A lot of my colleagues, their perception of camp is that they want kids to have a lot of things that are cutting-edge in terms of technology. Like photography. What we want to do is give them a twist of something they don't have access to at home."

How to Get Vacations Right

Most of us aren't wealthy enough to vacation regularly at the Four Seasons or the Ritz-Carlton. But for the parents who can afford to leave town in high style for every major vacation, there is often wariness about the expectations such trips set up. Such a feeling crept up on Stephanie Joss when she heard her two children, ages 8 and 10, comparing the merits of various Four Seasons resorts. Both she and her husband come from middle-class families. They've grown wealthy through long hours spent over two decades working in investment banking and the law. When they leave New York City during their limited time off, they want to treat themselves to hotel stays and experiences that are as relaxing and memorable as possible. Still, Joss can't quite shake the nagging question of whether her children need a bit of a reality reset.

Should parents who can afford to vacation in whatever way they want practice symbolic deprivation on their trips as well? The Josses are not all about five-star resorts and private guides. They've visited the Liberty Bell and toured Amish country. Their children also travel with relatives who don't have nearly as much money. On a recent trip to upstate New York, her son came back with stories about how much fun the motel was that they had stayed in with his aunt and grandmother. "It was great because it had a Coke machine," Joss said, recalling her son's excitement, "which the Four Seasons doesn't. If you want a Coke, you have to call and then they bring you a $50 Coke."

The soda encounter proves a larger point: However much adults may enjoy having hotel attendants bring them straw-berries and Evian spray poolside for a week or two each year, kids remember everyday experiences just as well, or even better. Here's one tactic that parents can use to deliver them: For every week you're at a resort try to take a day or part of one to get away from it. Figure out what local families do, and go do that.

Maybe it's the biggest playground or the most popular public pool. Farmers markets and other open-air bazaars offer all sorts of adventures; find food that no one in the family has ever eaten before, and persuade everyone to try it. Look up the local team that plays the most popular sport, and attend a game. Take the cheapest form of public transportation to get there. Traveling outside the United States? Wander around a grocery store for a while; kids observe all sorts of things about the local junk food that adults never notice. See if your friends have contacts in the area and get yourself invited to someone's home or neighborhood or workplace or block party.

Stephanie Joss's daughter has asked her whether traveling with her grandmother will mean waiting in lots of lines, or whether they'll have a guide who will arrange for them to skip the lines as they sometimes do when she goes with her parents. This question is one that plenty of vacationers face, given how many American amusement parks now allow families to pay a few hundred dollars more in exchange for a front-of-the-line pass for the day. Time is money, and the investment may make sense in purely economic terms for a family who wants to pack a lot into each trip.

But cutting in line is something one just doesn't do, and kids are particularly sensitive to that rule from an early age. Paying money to do it on vacation and marching right by the other kids in a park that's supposed to be full of amusements for all sends an awfully confusing message. Parents who plan to do it should at least explain the system to their kids ahead of time: Sometimes having more money means getting to do things that other families can't—and doing them in front of those very people. If that doesn't seem fair or it makes kids uncomfortable, then line jumping is probably not such a great idea after all.

One Family's Journey and a Case Study for Our Kids

As always, we're in the adult-making business here. The goal is not to make our children feel bad about whatever advantages they have or to shun those advantages as they grow older. Nor should parents feel as if they have to apologize to their kids or anyone else for their own good fortune. Having more than enough money is a great thing. What we don't want, however, are children who have no curiosity about people who are different from them and no understanding of what it might be like to have less. We're trying to imprint sensitivity and a lack of presumption that everyone is alike in their resources and the choices available to them.

This awareness is necessary because sometimes the differences among children aren't something they stop to consider. When Ruth Mendoza landed at Logan International Airport in Boston on January 11, 1987, she was a young woman from Bolivia whose mother had recently died. She spoke almost no English and was there to work as a babysitter for a family in suburban Needham. The arrangement was illegal, though she didn't know it at the time. Eventually, through the help of some kind neighbors of the family she first worked for, she found a better job. Not long after, she got married and obtained a green card.

Mendoza's new employers had high hopes for their child, enrolling her in the Meadowbrook School, a private junior-kindergarten-through-eighth-grade school in Weston, one of the wealthiest communities in the state. The school was beautiful, with gray-shingled Cape Cod–style buildings and rolling green athletic fields. By 1992, Ruth was going there every day to pick up the girl in her care. The family had high hopes for Ruth as well. They helped her with her budget, and she was eventually able to buy a used car. Crucially, they also allowed her to bring her own baby to her babysitting job, which helped her save money on daycare.

When it came time for Ruth to enroll her own daughter in school, the family she worked for asked her to consider something that hadn't even occurred to her: applying to Meadowbrook. "My first impression was no, I could never belong there as a parent," she said. "I tried to avoid the conversation. I remember missing the deadlines." A year later she finally applied, and she remembers the mixer for candidate families like it was yesterday. "Very fancy ladies, all dressed up, talking about things I couldn't quite relate to," she said. "I just thought, well, here I am, and these people seem very lovely and I'm sure their children are lovely, and this is one of only how many social screenings? That's when I realized we probably wouldn't get in."

But her daughter Melissa did get in, and the school embraced the family when she enrolled in 1996. They received enough financial aid that Ruth paid just $600 a year for tuition. She straddled the role of nanny picking up one student and parent tending another as best she could, and by 2002 she enrolled in a weekend program to try to earn the college degree she had been working toward for years. The next year, a job as an after-school teacher at Meadowbrook came up, and Ruth applied and got it. The schedule flexibility and benefits allowed her to finish her college degree in 2005, at which point something totally unexpected happened: The beloved kindergarten teacher who had taught both Ruth's daughter and her employer's daughter decided to retire. Meadowbrook gave the job to Ruth.

The transition from nanny to teacher was not without its challenges, but at least Ruth's status at the school had changed slowly over time. In the workplace, there was more pride than awkwardness in how far Ruth had come. Her daughters—three of them eventually—have remained on scholarship throughout their time there. And they feel their difference acutely. One daughter came home one day after a return from school vacation and asked, "Didn't you know we were supposed to go to Florida for a week?" No, Ruth replied, what made her think that? "Everyone went to Florida for a week," her daughter told her.

Some of the toughest slights, however, are more subtle, built as they are on hurtful assumptions and decisions that plenty of well-meaning teenagers make. Many schools allow kids to go out for lunch, which is potentially problematic. Some kids can go whenever and wherever they want without thinking about the cost. Others must bring their lunch every day because their families don't have anything left over for midday meals at Chipotle or Subway. And financial aid—even a full ride—doesn't include a stipend for off-campus meals.

One day Ruth picked one of her daughters up from the train and discovered that she was famished. What did she have for lunch? Nothing. So why didn't she eat? A friend at the high school she went to after Meadowbrook had asked her to come out with her for lunch, but she told the friend that she didn't have any money. The friend had some and said it would be no problem; she had another friend coming and was going to cover her, too. Off they went for bagels. Just as Ruth's daughter was about to order, her friend clarified the terms of the deal: She could just repay her tomorrow. At which point Ruth's daughter issued her own clarification: "No, you don't understand. I can't pay tomorrow, because tomorrow I'll have no money either. I thought I'd told you that I had no money."

What would we want our own kids to do in that situation? It's a small school. The families know one another. By the time the kids are going off campus for lunch, they're old enough to understand that some families have much more money than others and that they probably have classmates who can't afford much in the way of extras. Even if Ruth's daughter's friend didn't know that about the family, the revelation that she had no money to repay her should have changed the situation. They could have turned around and gone back to school to eat, so Ruth's daughter could have eaten the lunch that the school provides each day. Or her friend, who was not struggling financially herself, could have bought her lunch and told her not to worry about it.

On that day, however, neither of those things happened. The friends bought lunch only for themselves. And since school rules forbid the students from walking alone outside school property, Ruth's daughter couldn't just go back to campus right away. Instead, she had to watch her friends eat and then walk back to school with them. By the time they returned, it was too late for her to eat lunch in the cafeteria, since she had to go straight to class.

Ruth had a variety of mixed feelings when she heard the

story. "In the moment, you are angry," she said. "This may sound awful, but sometimes you accept that this is how it needs to be. My daughters are getting something that I could not afford, and some of their classmates are living such a sheltered life and can't see any other reality. It does make me wonder what else I'm missing, though. Kids only tell you so much."

So she let it go, and she takes pains to make it clear that she's not bitter about it. "This still feels like a dream to me," she said, sweeping her arms toward the well-equipped library where we were sitting, next to the classroom that she oversees. "That I am actually here and that this is my new reality, like somebody needs to pinch me."

Still, no parent ever wants their child to hurt another in this way. As I raise my own daughter, I think about this story often because someday, my daughter may be the friend with the lunch money. I want her to know what the right thing to do is, instinctively.

9

How Much Is Enough?

All about trade-offs

When I first started searching for parents with useful ideas about how to talk to kids about money, I was seeking two things. I wanted to find mothers and fathers who had acted on those ideas in unique ways. I also hoped to figure out what overarching philosophy or instinct was behind all their great ideas. There were plenty of people with good stories to tell about family rituals around spending, saving, giving, and talking about money. But there were very few with any kind of governing principle—a god, guru, book, question, or something else—that guided them when trying to use money to help teach their kids values.

I distinctly remember sitting in Keely and Mick Solimene's kitchen outside Chicago and asking them about this issue from every angle. How did her working-class upbringing, his work in investment banking, and their time in Barrington coalesce into a blueprint that led to their decision to downsize and pursue charitable work? I assumed that they had thought long and hard about all the decisions they had made along the way and how they would discuss them with their children.

So what did you stand for as a couple, I asked them, trying to get a bead on their own values and the character traits they cared about most. Blank stares.

How did you pick the town in the first place, the one you ended up leaving? Well, they said, it wasn't a decision about community so much as it was the best house they could get for the money they were willing to spend. "I don't remember its being anything more than that," Mick said.

What about the kids' allowance? Was it fairly regimented? "I don't think we really thought about it," he said. Indeed, they had four kids in six years before adopting two more many years later, so things were kind of busy.

What about the pressure of living in an affluent community and measuring yourself against what all the other families in town had or didn't have? "I could never even imagine keeping track of all those gadgets and where the kids landed in terms of their peers," Keely said. "There were no rules. All the kids were different. I'm beginning to sound like we're winging it here! But when you're a young couple raising your family, it's a new process and experience for everyone. Nobody who is raising children has done it before. It's a blank slate, and we're also growing and changing as we raise our children."

That last part is crucial. We know that kids change rapidly, and that each child is different from the last. The airtight method of getting the oldest kid to take the garbage out may fall flat with the youngest. Your child's best friends may have no urge to blow the contents of the Spend jar or drain their debit cards while you struggle to reprogram your kid to hang on to money for more than a week. And all the while, as we strive to be the ideal authority figures with sensible rules and explicit, illuminating explanations that open windows in our children's brains, we, too, are changing, trying to figure out what's most important to us and how to transmit those values to our kids.

Still, there is one crucial question that applies to nearly everything we've considered so far. In fact, it's one of the central questions of human happiness, productivity, and prudent financial planning, whether you're Bill Gates or down to the last dollar each month: How much is enough?

Defining Enough and Narrating
Your Spending Decisions

Kids aren't born with much self-restraint. From an early age, they'll take toys from others, eat sweets until they get sick, and stay out in the sun all day until they resemble lobsters. Later, they'll play video games until their eyes glaze over if we let them and stay up until the sun rises. Many of them seem programmed for risk and rule breaking, and they often drink alcohol years before it's legal and get drunk repeatedly and purposefully. They do these things because they can, because they're fun, because they're testing the limits of satisfaction and pleasure, going overboard fairly often.

But at the same time, as economist and parent Joshua Gans has noted, kids are acutely aware of the fact that the one economic law that most directly governs their lives is one of scarcity: There usually isn't enough to go around. That's why they have to fight for the toys or the swings or the cake piece with

Thomas's engine on it. By age 7 or 8, there are only so many spots on the travel soccer team or on a classmate's slumber party invitation list. Accelerated math class has just 15 kids in it, and many schools discourage more than a certain number of seniors to apply to Ivy League schools, so as not to lower the school's overall acceptance rate in admissions.

So kids are used to limits. In our homes, we want to set them within reason and do so consistently. This can be enormously challenging when many of the limits we set are completely artificial. Lots of us can afford to buy our kids more toys, treats, clothes, and gear than we actually do. Plenty of children want much more than we are willing to give them. Those of us who grew up with less than we have now may not be able to suppress the desire that our kids should want for nothing. *Won't*, as a Denver financial planner named Jonathan Duong puts it, requires much greater conviction than *can't*. And of course we want our kids to have the very best of what we do get them.

At the same time, we fear raising children who will think they have it all coming to them. So we end up imposing limits willy-nilly, ones that can sometimes be comedic. A favorite story of mine in this regard comes from a woman in Greenwich, Connecticut, whose family lives in a very substantial house. Despite their means, however, her husband refused to get a generator to keep the lights and air-conditioning on during long-lasting power outages. The kids, he explained to her, should know what it is to suffer. The idea of suffering in a mansion seems crazy, but plenty of parents create such internalized scoreboards with their own definitions of enough and then issue rulings without ever explaining their logic. Maybe that's because there isn't much of it.

One of the most profound challenges of having kids is that

raising them isn't simply about shaping their financial values and decision-making skills. Teaching them means questioning our own priorities as well, which is a healthy thing to do in any event. So defining *enough* for us grown-ups has to happen as early as possible in the parenting process. One good place to start is with a credit or debit card statement. For people who use cards often enough, the spending there can stand in for a large part of the household budget. So what does our budget say about our values? This question is a favorite of Carl Richards, who contributes sketches each week to *The New York Times* that illustrate how our feelings influence the way we handle money. After all, the list of things we spend money on is living proof of what we find valuable. Otherwise, why would we be spending money on it?

Try to identify categories where you spend the most discretionary money and consider which of the objects and outings brought you the most joy. Some of the cheapest meals create the most lasting memories. The line item for the deposit on last summer's lake house may make your head explode with memories of sunsets and smallmouth bass. Perhaps there is cable television that you don't watch anymore or subscriptions you don't read. Inevitably, there will be things you want to consume twice as much of next year and half as much of next month.

What themes do all these individual transactions add up to? Perhaps the thread running through the bill is that you value experiences over things, or collector's items more than clothes. Maybe incredible food is your highest priority, and you offset the cost with cheap furniture from IKEA. Or perhaps art is one of the biggest passions in your life and you spend heavily on that while economizing at home with lots of pasta. There are no wrong answers here as long as you're not spending more than you're making—but there may be themes that emerge that feel wrong to you when you look at it this way. And if your kids were to read the bills—and they'll eventually see them lying around or find one on a screen—what would they say is important to you? Would you feel good about their assessment?

If not, imagine how you'd want the conversation to go about your own financial choices and how your kids might relate to them at different ages. Say you're moving to another city for a new job. It may be for a higher salary, a lower cost of living, more satisfaction, or to be closer to family. Why wasn't the old wage sufficient? Were the housing prices in the last town too high? Just how important is it to be happy at work or live near grandparents or uncles and aunts? These are, at their essence, questions about how much is enough. So is the baseline you set for needs and wants when it comes to kids' athletic gear or clothing, as you decide whether you'll pay for new clothes at Target, Old Navy, Lands' End, Nike, Patagonia, or someplace even more expensive.

If your budget allows for growing opportunities to spend money on every child's favorite activities, you'll have ever more opportunities to narrate your spending decisions in these areas. At a certain point, we have to decide when every child has had enough lessons, coaching, tutoring, and summer camp. When you reach that point, talk with your kids about what you've spent so far and explain why it may be time to stop. It isn't always easy to articulate these issues, but we need the practice. After all, college is on the horizon, and many families face choices between private and public colleges that involve total price differences of more than $100,000. Many of us will ultimately need to be able to figure out how much education is enough and explain it to children who have their hearts set on the most expensive one of all.

A Word to Make Kids Wiser: Trade-Offs

We can't have or do everything we want, and it's a lesson we need to remind our kids of often. Even if there is enough money, there's not enough time. At its root, the question of how much is enough is reflected in choices we make nearly every day. And many of these choices are trade-offs.

Yoni Engelhart, who lives in Brookline, Massachusetts, with his wife and four children, has spent much of his adult life considering them. Like many business school students, examining case studies of businesses and nonprofit organizations was a major part of his two years of study toward an MBA. Managing trade-offs, he discovered, was at the core of organizational success. One example that stuck with him was that of a successful bank that decided to do just three things well: checking accounts, savings accounts, and customer service. It traded off higher potential profits in loans or serving business customers in exchange for the money it could make serving more consumers better than other banks. Another such model is Apple, a company that's chosen to compete in just a handful of product areas when consumers would no doubt try whatever other electronics it chose to manufacture.

Good living, he soon realized, is also about making good trade-offs. One of the most basic and yet emotionally complex trade-offs for adults is spending less now in order to have more money later. He wanted his kids to be considering that trade-off at the earliest possible age. So to create what he hoped would be an exciting alternative to consumption, he started a bank at his house (and on a Google spreadsheet) that pays about 20 percent in annual interest. That's enough so that when he credits it to the accounts each Sunday, even the kids with the smallest balances can see the number go up. Word got out in the neighborhood, and about 20 children now have money on deposit at the First Kids Bank of Brookline. One boy brings the change he finds in the street to Engelhart's house, where the money sits in plastic bags in a safe.

Engelhart has no problem with his children, the oldest of whom is 7, buying the things they want. His desire is simply that it be a considered choice. "It's changed the conversation around spending," he said. "Buying stuff is great but not buying stuff is also great, because you have the benefit of growing the money. So when they get a birthday check, their first instinct now isn't necessarily to go out and buy something. They may decide to put the money in the bank as quickly as possible so they definitely don't miss a Sunday."

The Engelharts have introduced trade-offs into other aspects of their children's lives as well. The family has established a toy equilibrium where any time a new one arrives on a birthday or through a purchase, an older one goes to the children's hospital where their mother, Talia, works. The Engelhart children understand that they have enough toys and that overall growth in their collection probably won't improve their lives all that much. So they think each time about which ones are most valuable, and whether a toy for playing outside that only gets used six or eight months out of the year is worth keeping.

The conversations extend to charity, and the two oldest children already get to decide where some of the family giving budget goes. Donations to a local food bank feed people directly and quickly, but donating an animal via an organization like Oxfam can help someone have milk and other dairy products for a long period of time, and meat later on. The kids decide how to split the funds among the two options.

Even seemingly unrelated matters can become part of the trade-off conversation. When the fourth Engelhart child was about to arrive, Yoni engaged the older children in a discussion about whether the family should replace a six-year-old stroller that was ratty but still functional or use the money to spend a few nights away in New Hampshire. This was a tough one: an experience they would enjoy versus a stroller that they would derive no benefit from. But his 7-year-old daughter informed him that the wheels don't lock the way they are supposed to and that their babysitter has a lot of trouble with turning as well. She was thinking about how she could make her sitter's life easier, and the inconvenience mattered to her. "I look for excuses to have these conversations because I think they're so rich," Yoni said. "It develops brain muscles that will serve them well in life, not just financially but certainly financially."

We should look for these opportunities, too. How much is enough, and what should we trade off so that we have all the things we need and enough of what we want to make us as happy as possible? It's a savings question when it comes to allowance. It's a spending question when it comes to helping kids learn to buy things that will give them the most utility and joy. It's a question of impact when giving money away and trying to maximize the good it does. When kids start earning, we want them to figure out how much they need and to what end. And when we reflect on what we have, we want our kids to grow into young adults with perspective—people with a healthy definition of enough that is unique to them and isn't based on what everyone else has or does.

That doesn't mean we have to talk about money all the time. Smarts, kindness, loyalty, health—these things come first. "I want them to be interested, but not obsessed," Engelhart explained. "I would be disappointed if this were the first thing they thought of each day."

So over the 20 years or so that our children live with us, we should try to have just enough conversations about money and the values behind our financial decisions. Only then will they have a complete picture of where we stand, what we stand for, and how we make financial decisions. Given how much we invest in them, talking about what we spend and save and give away, and why, is one of the important legacies we can leave them.

And so it is with my family. We have no idea whether our daughter will grow up to be a dancer or a banker. We have no control over how much money she will make. But we can influence how she will think about whatever she has by being honest about what we do with our own money now. She should know how to save but also how and when to splurge. She should know how to protect herself, too, from her own feelings about money and those of others who might manipulate her. It is an essential part of parenting, even more so than getting her ready for standardized tests or her driver's license exam.

We haven't got very long, and the years go by so quickly. Still, we have these conversations because they endure. They're an essential part of making successful adults—and contented ones too.

Acknowledgments

As I've gone about my reporting these last few years, friends and strangers have often asked me about the single most important thing I've learned. Turns out it wasn't a parenting tip per se. Instead, it's the enduring power of gratitude to give us perspective on our lives and make us happier overall. And I have so much to be grateful for.

This book was born of a couple of talks I gave to parents at the Abraham Joshua Heschel School in Manhattan and Berkeley Carroll School in Brooklyn. Thanks to Judith Shulevitz and Sophia Romero for inviting me and to the parents there for realizing that my work was adding up to something bigger before I did myself.

Because I subscribe to the newsletter of nonfiction book marketing guru Tim Grahl, who has taught me a ton and built me a very nice website, I knew to start creating a community around these topics on the day I sold the book. Thanks to Tim and Ken Kurson for helping me gather the tribe. Since then, thousands of people on my Facebook page have weighed in on matters large and small. It was yet another lesson in the fact that none of us is as smart as all of us; the distilled wisdom of the *Opposite of Spoiled* Facebook community is on almost every page of this book, and I'm so much wiser for having read every one of your comments.

To the members of the Invisible Institute, thank you for your unending generosity and collegiality. To the members of the Highly Visible Institute, thank you for the inspiration to bust through walls.

My editors at *The New York Times* have given me more freedom than I deserve to stretch the definition of personal finance about as far as it can go. Thanks to Larry Ingrassia and Bill Keller for bringing me in; Dean Murphy, Jill Abramson, and Dean Baquet for keeping me; and Phyllis Messinger, Jane Bornemeier, Cass Peterson, and her crew of copy aces for keeping me from embarrassing myself too often. Throughout my time there, Kevin McKenna has done more than nearly anyone to help me make an impact, and I'm also grateful to have had Adam Bryant, Kelly Couturier, Kevin Granville, Jose Lopez, Winnie O'Kelley, Claudia Payne, Jim Schachter, Lon Teter, and Vera Titunik in my corner. As this project was taking shape, KJ Dell'Antonia let me hang around the *Motherlode* blog, which allowed me to test ideas and get hammered when they weren't quite good enough. And thanks, as always, to the Sulzbergers and their descendants for making our work at the *Times* possible.

I'm doing what I do today thanks to Edward Felsenthal,

Dave Kansas, Jesse Pesta, and Eben Shapiro, who took me in at *The Wall Street Journal* 13 years ago. In the very best tradition of behind-the-scenes editors, Edward and Eben saw something in me that I never noticed in myself and nudged me toward the most fulfilling work of my career so far.

My fellow travelers and co-conspirators in personal finance in recent years have taught me so much about how to be more pointed, funny, skeptical, and humane. Praise be to Irina Aleksander, Ann Carrns, Sam Grobart, Mary Pilon, Carl Richards, Jennifer Saranow Schultz, Paul Sullivan, Nadia Taha, and Tanzina Vega. I'm proud of this book, but I'm not sure if anything can top the feeling of satisfaction I've gotten from working with Tara Siegel Bernard over the years to expose the unequal financial treatment of gay families.

Valerie Lapinski didn't think twice when I wanted to rent her second bedroom as an office, and she proved to be one of the best roommates I've ever had. Amato Nocera tracked down *Family Guy* scripts and obscure academic articles, and always had faith that it was all going to add up to something. Elizabeth Lefever helped me build an incredible list of books for kids of all ages about money and social class; look for it on my website soon. And Steve Burwell, Heidie Joo, and Alan Wenker put their eyes to parts or all of the manuscript and asked me tough questions of all sorts.

You will find my agent Christy Fletcher on Wikipedia under the "Has It All, Does It All, Wins the Day, Has Fun Doing it, Generalized Ass-kicker" entry. It's a joy to watch her work and to see the wheels of her brain turn as she cuts through nonsense and makes amazing things happen. Sylvie Greenberg in

Christy's office handles speaking requests three times as well as I ever did and four times as well as most of the lecture agents with five times her experience.

When Christy and I sat down to plot this project, Gail Winston was on top of our list of hoped-for editors. It felt like too much to wish for, getting to work with someone who still puts (lots of) red pen to paper over repeated drafts and knows exactly how to make a book like this help readers most. I've been blessed by her experience, patience, and keen ear for tone and tone-deafness. Maya Ziv answered every insane question and lapped me at various road races just to keep me in my place, and Emily Cunningham ably picked up where Maya left off. Thanks also to Stephanie Cooper and Leah Wasielewski for the ace marketing work, and Kathy Schneider for air cover. Leslie Cohen was kind enough to entertain all my nutty publicity ideas without laughing too hard. As you read this, Leslie, I intend to be living in a sleeping bag in your office, just so you know.

My 40-year-old collection of dozens of loyal friends took a keen interest in this book, and I felt intensely lucky every time you told me your stories, asked about my latest discovery, and tolerated my rambling soliloquies over dinners and at drop-offs. A special thanks to my Chicago, Amherst, and Brooklyn people for your unending enthusiasm and support.

The use of the terms *we* and *us* throughout this book is meant solely in the spirit of community building. Blame not my parents, siblings, or other relatives for any unconvincing pronouncements. Please do, however, credit my father, Fred, with seeding my first mutual fund investment and my mother, Charlene, for letting me tag along on the financial-aid negotiation journey. My siblings, Stephanie and David, and I are solvent and (mostly) sane, thanks to what we picked up from them along the way. My in-laws, Wendy and Harry Kantor, remain a model of unending generosity. And I could not do what I do without Donna Mitchell. Thanks to her, I never worry about my daughter for a single second when my wife and I are not around.

And Jodi. Nothing makes me happier than all the things we get to do together. In the newsroom, my best friend is a staircase away. On rides home over this long stretch, you've taken my words and made them sound more like me without needing to ask what I'm trying to say. It seems miraculous when it happens, yet it happens all the time.

Our most joyful joint effort, meanwhile, continues. Talia, as lonely as reporting and writing can sometimes be, I thought of you happily as your chalk drawings on the wall behind me and your painted banners on the wall in front of me urged me on. Your every question is thrilling; please don't ever stop asking them. Thank you for being my pride and joy and test subject and inspiration. I am the luckiest.

Notes

1 | Why We Need to Talk About Money

6   *This shift—moving the risk and the economic burden from employers to workers—has taken decades . . . but it's now nearly complete.* Hacker, *The Great Risk Shift.*

7   *One comparison of the earnings.* Data compiled by Bhashkar Mazumder, senior economist at the Federal Reserve Bank of Chicago, and Jonathan Davis, a University of Chicago doctoral student, at the request of the author, 2013.

8   *epidemic of silence.* Several of the questions in this chapter are inspired by similar ones asked in Furnham, *Economic Socialisation of Young People,* 158–203.

10   *the assembled writings.* Fogarty, *Overindulged Children: A Parent's Guide,* and Fogarty, *Overindulged Children and the Adults They Become.*

11   *A 1998 academic journal article.* David J. Bredehoft et al., "Perceptions Attributed by Adults to Parental Overindulgence During Childhood," *Journal of Family and Consumer Sciences Education,* vol. 16, no. 2, Fall/Winter, 1998, 7.

2 | How to Start the Money Conversations

17   *describes in his memoir.* "Cheerful Money," Friend, *Cheerful Money*, 96.

18   *described childhood innocence.* Schor, *Born to Buy*, 15.

20   *described the potential predicament this way.* Fogarty, *Over-indulged Children: Parent's Guide*, 96.

21   *our daughter had put it together.* The Haggadah my daughter made was based on Francine Hermeline Levite's *My Haggadah: Made It Myself* (New York: Made It Myself Books, 2012).

21   *"place of intrigue."* Simon, *Moral Questions in the Classroom*, 16.

24   *A number of polls and studies.* Charles Schwab . . . released the survey on May 24, 2011, and it has not produced a similar one since. The data I cited is accessible here: http://bit .ly/1aLRYOo.

31   *an* authoritarian *parent.* This framing comes from Baumrind, "Authoritative Parenting for Character and Competence," in *Parenting for Character*, 17.

38   *But when I wrote about the "How much do you make?" question. New York Times, Motherlode* blog, "What to Do When Your Child Asks About Your Income," last modified October 13, 2013, http://bucks.blogs.nytimes.com/2010/07/20/ kids-money-questions-why-is-that-person-asking-for-money/.

3 | The Allowance Debates

47   *a 2011 one out of New Zealand.* Terrie E. Moffitt et al., "A gradient of childhood self-control predicts health, wealth, and public safety," *Proceedings of the National Academy of*

Sciences of the United States of America, vol. 108, no. 7, 2011, 2–3, doi:1073/pnas.1010076108.

54   as David Owen put it. Owen, *Bank of Dad.*

66   The American Institute of Certified Public Accountants ran a survey. The survey was released on August 22, 2012, http://www.aicpa.org/press/pressreleases/2012/pages/aicpa-survey-reveals-what-parents-pay-kids-for-allowance-grades.aspx.

66   T. Rowe Price ran its own survey. The survey was released on July 3, 2012. The allowance data is on slide 25, http://media.moneyconfidentkids.com/wp-content/uploads/2012/03/PKM-Survey-Results-Additional-Slides-FINAL-07-03-12.pdf.

67   Blanche Dismorr used data she drew. Blanche Dismorr, "Ought Children to Be Paid for Domestic Services?" in *Studies in Education, 1896–1902,* vol. 2, Earl Barnes, ed., Publisher unknown, 1902, http://bit.ly/1f5LuBd.

69   he wrote in an online essay. Jake Johnson, "Raising Entrepreneurs: Fostering the entrepreneurial spirit in your kids," Medium, 2013, http://bit.ly/1lovUB1.

4 | The Smartest Ways for Kids to Spend

73   What's been lost over the years. The connection between thrift and thriving originates in Yates and Hunter, *Thrift and Thriving.*

76   Which one does the most good and the least harm? Weil, *Power and Promise,* 16.

77   "Are we exclusionary? Absolutely." Benoit Denizet-Lewis, "The Man Behind Abercrombie & Fitch," *Salon,* January 24, 2006, http://www.salon.com/2006/01/24/jeffries/.

5 | Are We Raising Materialistic Kids?

92   *"once reserved for royalty."* Damon, *Greater Expectations,* 14.

92   *never had a hot shower.* Kasser, *High Price of Materialism,* 58.

93   *"economy of dignity."* Pugh, *Longing and Belonging,* 6.

93   *"a sort of unwelcome invisibility."* Ibid., 18.

93   *"matching."* Ibid., 51.

93   *"patrolling."* Ibid., 69.

94   *"dignity gauntlet."* Ibid., 96.

94   *"full provisioning."* Ibid., 98.

94   *And the fallout is unpleasant in countries all over the world.* Tim Kasser has catalogued the ill effects, which include higher levels of depression and anxiety; headaches, backaches, sore muscles, and sore throats; more drinking, pot smoking, and use of hard drugs; social isolation; separation from one's parents; attention deficit disorder; paranoia; aggressiveness in dating relationships; Machiavellianism; and the desire to hang out with like-minded materialists. These correlated traits turn up in young people and old people; wealthy people and poor people; and among Romanians, South Koreans, and Danes, among many others. Kasser, *High Price of Materialism,* 5–22.

95   *One of the most eye-opening studies.* Marvin E. Goldberg and Gerald J. Gorn, "Some Unintended Consequences of TV Advertising to Children," *Journal of Consumer Research,* vol. 5, no. 1, June 1978, 22–29.

103   *declared the rising handout a bubble.* Dan Kadlec, "Baby-Tooth Bubble: Has the Tooth Fairy Lost Her Mind? *Time,* August 30, 2013, http://business.time.com/2013/08/30/baby-tooth-bubble-has-the-tooth-fairy-lost-her-mind.

103 *wrote about his disgust.* Bruce Feiler, "Curtain Up on Act II
for the Tooth Fairy," *New York Times*, December 9, 2011, ST2,
http://www.nytimes.com/2011/12/11/fashion/act-ii-for-the-
tooth-fairy-this-life.html.

112 *decided to find out.* Tim Kasser, Katherine L. Rosenblum,
Arnold J. Samaroff, Edward L. Deci, et al., "Changes in materialism, changes in psychological well-being: Evidence from
three longitudinal studies and an intervention experiment,"
Motivation and Emotion, vol. 38, no. 1, February 2014, 1–22,
doi 10.1007/s11031-013-9371-4.

6 | How to Talk About Giving

119 *ran a poll.* Themint.org Poll: Kids Are Clueless About Parents' Charitable Giving, last modified December 22, 2010,
http://www.northwesternmutual.com/news-room/122629.

120 *research on happiness shows.* Dunn and Norton, *Happy
Money*, 109–10.

121 *One delightful study that makes this point is.* Lara B. Aknin,
J. Kiley Hamlin, Elizabeth W. Dunn, "Giving Leads to Happiness in Young Children," June 14, 2012, *PloS ONE* 7(6):
e39211, doi:10.1371/journal.pone.0039211.

124 *according to Susan Engel.* Susan Engel, "Open Pandora's Box:
Curiosity and Imagination in the Classroom (The Thomas H.
Wright Lecture, Child Development Institute, Sarah Lawrence
College, Summer 2006), http://issuu.com/gfbertini/docs/
open_pandora_s_box_-_curiosity_and_imagination_in_/1.

126 *a blog post I wrote.* Children's Money Questions: Why Is That
Person Asking for Money?, last modified October 13, 2013,
http://bucks.blogs.nytimes.com/2010/07/20/kids-money-
questions-why-is-that-person-asking-for-money/.

126   *put it in their book.* Gallo and Gallo, *Silver Spoon Kids*, 155.

130   *somebody else is watching.* Kristin L. Leimgruber et al., "Young Children Are More Generous When Others Are Aware of Their Actions," October 31, 2012, *PLoS ONE* 7(10): e48292, doi:10.1371/journal.pone.0048292.

131   *About one-third of all charitable donations.* Giving USA Study, 2014, http://www.philanthropy.iupui.edu/news/article/ giving-usa-2014.

136   *a large Mercedes.* Salwen and Salwen, *The Power of Half,* 24–25.

136   *"Soulless."* Ibid., 36.

136   *she asked her daughter.* Ibid., 32.

7 | Why Kids Should Work

151   *as Princeton sociologist Viviana A. Zelizer wrote.* Zelizer, *Priceless Child*, 4–5.

154   *is the answer to this question.* Angela L. Duckworth et al., "Grit: Perseverance and Passion for Long-Term Goals," *Journal of Personality and Social Psychology*, vol. 92, no. 6 (2007), 1087–1101, http://www.sas.upenn.edu/~duckwort/ images/Grit%20JPSP.pdf.

154   *a short essay that appeared in 2013.* Angela L. Duckworth and Lauren Eskreis-Winkler, "True Grit," *The Association for Psychological Science Observer*, vol. 26, no. 4, April 2013, 1, http://www.psychologicalscience.org/index.php/publications/ observer/2013/april-13/true-grit.html.

155   *a drive for competence.* Damon, *Greater Expectations*, 128–30.

155   *default to the assumption.* Ibid., 36.

156   *who filled me in on the backstory.* These quotes are taken from a post I wrote for the *Dinner: A Love Story* blog on

November 8, 2013, http://www.dinneralovestory.com/how-young-is-too-young/.

156 *"honorable Mealtime."* The quotes that follow are from Reid, *Confucius Lives Next Door,* 147–49.

157 *In national surveys.* Damon, *Greater Expectations,* 37.

8 | The Luckiest

173 *she showed 3-year-olds a series.* Patricia G. Ramsey, "Young Children's Awareness and Understanding of Social Class Differences," *Journal of Genetic Psychology,* vol. 152, no. 1, 1990, 71–82, doi: 10.1080/00221325.1991.9914679.

175 *found strong correlations.* Jeffrey J. Froh et al., "Gratitude and the Reduced Costs of Materialism in Adolescents," *Journal of Happiness Studies,* vol. 12, no. 2, 2010, 289–302, doi 10.1007/s10902-010-9195-9, people.hofstra.edu/jeffrey_j_froh/spring%202010%20web/10.1007_s10902-010-9195-9[1].pdf.

175 *a series of experimental "gratitude interventions."* The Greater Good Science Center at the University of California, Berkeley, has a list of links to various gratitude studies about adults and children, http://bit.ly/1huxqPw.

175 *Homer wrote.* As cited in Henry Lancelot Dixon, *"Saying Grace" Historically Considered: And Numerous Forms of Grace Taken from Ancient and Modern Sources; with Appendices* (Oxford: James Parker and Co., 1903), 3.

175 *Deuteronomy 8:10 commands.* As referenced by the online Bible Gateway, http://bit.ly/1as4brq.

175 *An Egyptian inscription.* A. M. Blackman, "The King of Egypt's Grace Before Meat," *Journal of Egyptian Archaeology,* vol. 31, 1945, 57–73.

175 *Just 44 percent.* Robert D. Putnam and David E. Campbell, *American Grace: How Religion Unites and Divides Us* (New York: Simon & Schuster, 2010), 10.

177 *"not-so-public" schools.* Pugh, *Longing and Belonging,* 179.

181 *At Manhattan Country School.* Some of the descriptions of the school's home visits program come from a column I wrote about it. Ron Lieber, "For Lessons About Class, a Field Trip Takes Students Home," *New York Times,* May 31, 2014, B1, http://www.nytimes.com/2014/05/31/your-money/for-lessons-about-social-class-a-field-trip-takes-students-right-back-home.html?_r=0.

185 *a post I'd written.* Ron Lieber, "A Daughter, Her Dad, and the Debate Over Pricey Teen Volunteer Trips," last modified March 6, 2014, http://parenting.blogs.nytimes.com/2014/03/06/a-daughter-her-dad-and-the-debate-over-pricey-teen-volunteer-trips/.

185 *a post that she had written to explain.* "The Problem with Little White Girls and Boys," last modified February 18, 2014, http://pippabiddle.com/2014/02/18/the-problem-with-little-white-girls-and-boys/.

187 *"symbolic deprivation."* Pugh, *Longing and Belonging,* 9.

9 | How Much Is Enough?

201 *Joshua Gans has noted.* Gans, *Parentonomics,* 145.

Bibliography

These are the books that had the biggest impact on me as I was preparing to write. You'll find essential wisdom in every one of them.

Aries, Elizabeth, with Richard Berman. *Speaking of Race and Class: The Student Experience at an Elite College.* Philadelphia: Temple University Press, 2013.

Baumeister, Roy F., and John Tierney. *Willpower: Rediscovering the Greatest Human Strength.* New York: The Penguin Press, 2011.

Baumrind, Diana, et al. *Parenting for Character: Five Experts, Five Practices.* Portland, Oregon: The Council for Spiritual and Ethical Education, 2008.

Bissonnette, Zac. *How to Be Richer, Smarter, and Better-Looking Than Your Parents.* New York: Portfolio, 2012.

Bronson, Po, and Ashley Merryman. *Nurture Shock: New Thinking About Children.* New York: Twelve, 2009.

Brosnan, Michael, editor. *The Inclusive School: A Selection of Writing on Diversity Issues in Independent Schools.* Washington, D.C.: The National Association of Independent Schools, 2012.

Calhoun, Ada. *Instinctive Parenting: Trusting Ourselves to Raise Good Kids*. New York: Gallery Books, 2010.

Coles, Robert. *The Moral Life of Children*. New York: Atlantic Monthly Press, 1986.

Damon, William. *Greater Expectations: Overcoming the Culture of Indulgence in Our Homes and Schools*. New York: Free Press, 1995.

——. *The Moral Child: Nurturing Children's Natural Moral Growth*. New York: Free Press, 1988.

Dungan, Nathan. *Money Sanity Solutions: Linking Money + Meaning*. Minneapolis: Share Save Spend, 2010.

Dunn, Elizabeth, and Michael Norton. *Happy Money: The Science of Smarter Spending*. New York: Simon & Schuster, 2013.

Durband, Dorothy B., and Sonya L. Britt, editors. *Student Financial Literacy: Campus-Based Program Development*. New York: Springer, 2012.

Dweck, Carol. *Mindset: The New Psychology of Success*. New York: Ballantine, 2006.

Eisner, Michael. *Camp*. New York: Warner Books, 2005.

Eyre, Linda, and Richard Eyre. *Teaching Your Children Values*. New York: Fireside, 1993.

Feiler, Bruce. *The Secrets of Happy Families: Improve Your Mornings, Rethink Family Dinner, Fight Smarter, Go Out and Play, and Much More*. New York: William Morrow, 2013.

Fogarty, James A. *Overindulged Children: A Parent's Guide to Mentoring*. Egg Harbor, New Jersey: Liberty Publishing Group, 2003.

——. *Overindulged Children and the Adults They Become: Narcissistic, Antisocial and Dependent Behaviors*. Brentwood, Tennessee: Cross Country Education, 2009.

Friend, Tad. *Cheerful Money: Me, My Family, and the Last Days of Wasp Splendor*. New York: Little Brown, 2009.

Froymovich, Riva. *End of the Good Life: How the Financial Crisis*

Threatens a Lost Generation and What We Can Do About It.
New York: Harper Perennial, 2013.

Furnham, Adrian. *The Economic Socialisation of Young People.*
London: The Social Affairs Unit, 2008.

Fussell, Paul. *Class: A Guide Through the American Status System.*
New York: Touchstone, 1992.

Galinsky, Ellen. *Mind in the Making: The Seven Essential Life Skills*
Every Child Needs. New York: William Morrow, 2010.

Gallo, Eileen, and John Gallo. *The Financially Intelligent Parent:*
Eight Steps to Raising Successful, Generous, Responsible Chil-
dren. New York: New American Library, 2005.

——. *Silver Spoon Kids: How Successful Children Raise Responsi-*
ble Children. New York: McGraw Hill, 2002.

Gans, Joshua. *Parentonomics: An Economist Dad Looks at Parent-*
ing. Cambridge, Massachusetts: The MIT Press, 2009.

Godfrey, Joline. *Raising Financially Fit Kids.* Berkeley, California:
Ten Speed Press, 2013.

Godfrey, Neale S., and Carolina Edwards. *Money Doesn't Grow on*
Trees: A Parent's Guide to Raising Financially Responsible
Children. New York: Fireside, 2006.

Grant, Ruth W. *Strings Attached: Untangling the Ethics of Incen-*
tives. New York: Russell Sage Foundation, 2012.

Hacker, Jacob. *The Great Risk Shift: The New Economic Insecurity*
and the Decline of the American Dream. New York: Oxford University Press, 2008.

Hausner, Lee. *Children of Paradise: Successful Parenting for Pros-*
perous Families. Irvine, California: Plaza Press, 2005.

Hoefle, Vicki. *Duct Tape Parenting: A Less Is More Approach to*
Raising Respectful, Responsible, and Resilient Kids. Brookline,
Massachusetts: Bibliomotion, 2012.

hooks, bell. *Where We Stand: Class Matters.* New York: Routledge,
2000.

Hulbert, Ann. *Raising America: Experts, Parents, and a Century of Advice About Children*. New York: Vintage, 2003.

Kasser, Tim. *The High Price of Materialism*. Cambridge, Massachusetts: The MIT Press, 2002.

Kobliner, Beth. *Get a Financial Life: Personal Finance in Your Twenties and Thirties*. New York: Simon & Schuster, 2009.

Kurson, Ken. *The Green Magazine Guide to Personal Finance: A No B.S. Money Book for Your Twenties and Thirties*. New York: Main Street Books, 1998.

Labanowski, Phyllis, and Pamela Freeman. *Created Equal: A Curriculum for High Schoolers and Middle Schoolers on Class and Classism*. Jamaica Plain, Massachusetts: Class Action, 2012.

Lamb, Sabrina. *Do I Look Like an ATM? A Parent's Guide to Raising Financially Responsible African American Children*. Chicago: Lawrence Hill Books, 2013.

Lareau, Annette. *Unequal Childhoods: Class, Race, and Family Life*. Berkeley: University of California Press, 2011.

Levine, Madeline. *The Price of Privilege: How Parental Pressure and Material Advantage Are Creating a Generation of Disconnected and Unhappy Kids*. New York: HarperCollins, 2006.

Lickona, Thomas. *Character Matters: How to Help Our Children Develop Good Judgment, Integrity, and Other Essential Virtues*. New York: Touchstone, 2004.

Livingston, James. *Against Thrift: Why Consumer Culture Is Good for the Economy, the Environment, and Your Soul*. New York: Basic Books, 2011.

McElwain, Sarah, editor. *Saying Grace: Blessings for the Family Table*. San Francisco: Chronicle Books, 2003.

McKinley, Kevin. *Make Your Kid a Millionaire: 11 Easy Ways Anyone Can Secure a Child's Financial Future*. New York: Fireside, 2002.

Mellan, Olivia. *Money Harmony: Resolving Money Conflicts in*

Your Life and Relationships. New York: Walker and Company, 1994.

Mogel, Wendy. *The Blessing of a Skinned Knee: Using Jewish Teachings to Raise Self-Reliant Children*. New York: Scribner, 2001.

Nagler, Tim. *Pine Island Camp: The First One Hundred Years*. Belgrade Lakes, Maine: Pine Island Camp, 2002.

Nucci, Larry. *Nice Is Not Enough: Facilitating Moral Development*. Upper Saddle River, New Jersey: Merrill, 2009.

Olen, Helaine. *Pound Foolish: Exposing the Dark Side of the Personal Finance Industry*. New York: Portfolio, 2013.

Opdyke, Jeff D. *Financially Ever After: The Couples' Guide to Managing Money*. New York: Collins Business, 2009.

Owen, David. *The First National Bank of Dad: The Best Ways to Teach Kids About Money*. New York: Simon & Schuster, 2003.

Paul, Pamela. *Parenting, Inc.: How the Billion-Dollar Baby Business Has Changed the Way We Raise Our Children*. New York: Times Books, 2008.

Perry, Ellen Miley. *A Wealth of Possibilities: Navigating Family, Money, and Legacy*. Washington, D.C.: Egremont Press, 2012.

Pink, Daniel H. *Drive: The Surprising Truth About What Motivates Us*. New York: Riverhead, 2009.

———. *To Sell Is Human: The Surprising Truth About Moving Others*. New York: Riverhead, 2013.

Power, F. Clark, Ann Higgins, and Lawrence Kohlberg. *Lawrence Kohlberg's Approach to Moral Education*. New York: Columbia University Press, 1989.

Price, Susan Crites. *The Giving Family: Raising Our Children to Help Others*. Washington, D.C.: Council on Foundations, 2003.

Pugh, Allison J. *Longing and Belonging: Parents, Children, and Consumer Culture*. Berkeley: University of California Press, 2009.

Reid, T. R. *Confucius Lives Next Door: What Living in the East Teaches Us About Living in the West.* New York: Vintage, 1999.

Richards, Carl. *The Behavior Gap: Simple Ways to Stop Doing Dumb Things with Money.* New York: Portfolio, 2012.

Roth, Geneen. *Lost and Found: Unexpected Revelations About Food and Money.* New York: Viking, 2011.

Rubin, Gretchen. *The Happiness Project: Or, Why I Spent a Year Trying to Sing in the Morning, Clean My Closets, Fight Right, Read Aristotle, and Generally Have More Fun.* New York: HarperCollins, 2011.

Salwen, Kevin, and Hannah Salwen. *The Power of Half: One Family's Decision to Stop Taking and Start Giving Back.* New York: Mariner, 2011.

Schor, Juliet B. *Born to Buy.* New York: Scribner, 2004.

Schulman, Michael. *Building Moral Communities: A Guide for Educators.* Portland, Oregon: The Council for Spiritual and Ethical Education, 2006.

Sethi, Ramit. *I Will Teach You to Be Rich.* New York: Workman, 2009.

Siegel, Judith P. *What Children Learn from Their Parents' Marriage.* New York: HarperCollins, 2000.

Simon, Katherine G. *Moral Questions in the Classroom: How to Get Kids to Think Deeply About Real Life and Their Schoolwork.* New Haven, Connecticut: Yale University Press, 2001.

Singer, Peter. *The Life You Can Save: Acting Now to End World Poverty.* New York: Random House, 2008.

Stanley, Thomas J., and William D. Danko. *The Millionaire Next Door: The Surprising Secrets of America's Wealthy.* New York: Pocket Books, 1996.

Streit, David, editor. *Good Things to Do: Expert Suggestions for Fostering Goodness in Kids.* Portland, Oregon: The Council for Spiritual and Ethical Education, 2009.

———. *Parenting for Character: Five Experts, Five Practices*. Portland, Oregon: The Council for Spiritual and Ethical Education, 2008.

Tough, Paul. *How Children Succeed: Grit, Curiosity, and the Hidden Power of Character*. New York: Houghton Mifflin Harcourt, 2012.

Ulrich, Carmen Wong. *The Real Cost of Living: Making the Best Choices for You, Your Life, and Your Money*. New York: Perigee, 2010.

Weber, Lauren. *In Cheap We Trust: The Story of a Misunderstood Virtue*. New York: Back Bay Books, 2009.

Weil, Zoe. *The Power and Promise of Humane Education*. Gabriola Island, British Columbia: New Society Publishers, 2004.

Weston, Liz Pulliam. *Easy Money: How to Simplify Your Finances and Get What You Want Out of Life*. New York: Financial Times Books, 2007.

Yates, Joshua J., and James Davidson Hunter, editors. *Thrift and Thriving in America: Capitalism and Moral Order from the Puritans to the Present*. New York: Oxford University Press, 2011.

Zelizer, Viviana A. *Pricing the Priceless Child: The Changing Social Value of Children*. Princeton, New Jersey: Princeton University Press, 1985.

Index

About the Author

RON LIEBER is the "Your Money" columnist for *The New York Times* and a contributor to the *Motherlode* parenting blog on nytimes.com. Before coming to *The Times*, he wrote a personal finance column for *The Wall Street Journal* and was on the staff of *Fortune* and *Fast Company* magazines. His first book, *Taking Time Off: Inspiring Stories of Students Who Enjoyed Successful Breaks from College and How You Can Plan Your Own*, coauthored with Colin Hall, was a *New York Times* bestseller in 1996. He lives in Brooklyn with his wife and daughter.

Ron speaks often to schools and community groups about parenting, money, and values. To learn more, and to sign up for his newsletter, visit ronlieber.com.